About Reading Connection:

Welcome to RBP Books' Connection series. Reading Connection provides students with focused practice to help reinforce and develop reading skills in areas appropriate for third-grade students. Reading Connection uses a variety of writing types and exercises to help build comprehension, thinking, phonics, vocabulary, language, reasoning, and other skills important to both reading and critical thinking. In accordance with NCTE (National Council of Teachers of English) standards, reading material and exercises are grade-level appropriate, and clear examples and instructions guide the lessons. Activities help students develop reading skills and give special attention to vocabulary development.

Dear Parents and Educators,

Thank you for choosing this Rainbow Bridge Publishing educational product to help teach your children and students. We take great pride and pleasure in becoming involved with your educational experience. Some people say that math will always be math and reading will always be reading, but we do not share that opinion. Reading, math, spelling, writing, geography, science, history, and all other subjects will always be some of life's most fulfilling adventures and should be taught with passion both at home and in the classroom. Because of this, we at Rainbow Bridge Publishing associate the greatness of learning with every product we create.

It is our mission to provide materials that not only explain, but also amaze; not only review, but also encourage; not only guide, but also lead. Every product contains clear, concise instructions, appropriate sample work, and engaging, grade-appropriate content created by classroom teachers and writers that is based on national standards to support your best educational efforts. We hope you enjoy our company's products as you embark on your adventure. Thank you for bringing us along.

Sincerely,

George Starks
Associate Publisher
Rainbow Bridge Publishing

Reading Connection™ • Grade 3
Written by Nancy Bosse and Deborah Morris

Publisher
Scott G. Van Leeuwen

Associate Publisher
George Starks

Series Creator
Michele Van Leeuwen

Illustrations
Amanda Sorensen

Visual Design and Layout
Andy Carlson, Robyn Funk, Zachary Johnson,
Dante J. Orazzi

Editorial Director
Paul Rawlins

Copy Editors and Proofreaders
Kim Carlson, Suzie Ellison, Melody Feist, Linda Swain

Please visit our website at
www.summerbridgeactivities.com
for supplements, additions, and corrections to this book.

Second Edition 2004

For orders call 1-800-598-1441
Discounts available for quantity orders

ISBN: 1-887923-82-9

PRINTED IN THE UNITED STATES OF AMERICA
10 9 8 7 6 5 4 3 2

Table of Contents

Sounds and Letters Chart

r(a)t   j(a)r   (b)ear   (c)at   (d)eer

(e)lephant   s(ea)l   f(er)n   (f)ish   (g)orilla

(h)orse   (i)nchworm   crocod(i)l(e)   b(ir)d   (j)aguar

(k)angaroo   (kn)ot   (l)ion   (m)ouse   (n)ewt

go(ng)   (o)ctopus   g(oo)se   cl(ou)d   (p)ig

(qu)ail   (r)abbit   (s)un   (sh)ark   (t)urtle

(th)in   d(u)ck   vult(ur)e   (v)ase   (w)olf

(wh)ale   fo(x)   (y)ak   pon(y)   (z)ebra

3rd Grade Reading List

Adler, David
Cam Jansen and the Mystery of the
Television Dog

Barrett, Judi
Cloudy with a Chance of Meatballs

Berenstain, Stan and Jan
Berenstain Bears—Chapter Books
Accept No Substitutes
And the Dress Code
And the New Girl in Town
And the Wheelchair Commando
. . . and others

Brown, Jeff
Flat Stanley

Burton, Virginia Lee
Katy and the Big Snow

Catling, Patrick Skene
Chocolate Touch

Cherry, Lynne
Great Kapok Tree: A Tale of the
Amazon Rain Forest

Cleary, Beverly
Ramona Quimby: Age 8

Cole, Joanna
Magic School Bus:
Inside the Earth
Magic School Bus:
Inside the Human Body
Magic School Bus:
On the Ocean Floor
. . . and others

Cooney, Barbara
Miss Rumphius

Dalgliesh, Alice
Courage of Sarah Noble

Danziger, Paula
There's a Bat in Bunk Five

DePaola, Tomie
Legend of the Bluebonnet

Donnelly, Judy
Wall of Names:
Story of the Vietnam Veterans Memorial
Who Shot the President? The Death of John
F. Kennedy
Moonwalk: First Trip to the Moon

Dorros, Arthur
Abuela

Ernst, Lisa Campbell
Nattie Parson's Good Luck Lamb

Fox, Paula
Maurice's Room

Gleiter, Jan
Paul Revere

Graff, Stewart
Helen Keller: Toward the Light

Gutelle, Andrew
Baseball's Best: Five True Stories

Havill, Juanita
Treasure Nap

Hidaka, Masako
Girl from the Snow Country

Jeschke, Susan
Perfect the Pig

Jonas, Ann
Aardvarks, Disembark!

3rd Grade Reading List

Jukes, Mavis
Blackberries in the Dark

Kellogg, Steven
Paul Bunyan
Best Friends

Konigsburg, E. L.
The View from Saturday

Krensky, Stephen
Witch Hunt

Lindgren, Astrid
Pippi Goes on Board

Little, Emily
Trojan Horse: How the Greeks
Won the War

Lobel, Arnold
Grasshopper on the Road
Book of Pigericks

Manes, Stephen
Be a Perfect Person in Just Three
Days

McCloskey, Robert
Homer Price

McMullan, Kate
Dinosaur Hunters

O'Connor, Jim
Jackie Robinson and the Story of All-
Black Baseball

Osborne, Mary Pope
Moonhorse

Peet, Bill
Spooky Tail of Prewitt Peacock
Wump World

Raskin, Ellen
Nothing Ever Happens on My Block

Schroeder, Alan
Minty: A Story of Young Harriet Tubman

Sharmat, Marjorie Weinman
Nate the Great series

Smith, Robert Kimmel
Chocolate Fever

Sobol, Donald J.
Encyclopedia Brown series

Stadler, John
Animal Cafe

Steig, William
The Amazing Bone
Amos and Boris
Sylvester and the Magic Pebble

Stock, Catherine
Emma's Dragon Hunt

Stoutenburg, Adrien
American Tall Tales

Waber, Bernard
Lyle, Lyle, Crocodile

Walter, Mildred Pitts
Justin and the Best Biscuits in the World

Whelan, Gloria
Next Spring an Oriole

White, E. B.
Charlotte's Web

Teach Me

Don't tell me that I can't, or I won't.
Always tell me to try, and I will.

Teach me to smile when I am sad.
Teach me to talk when I am mad.

Teach me to soar and teach me to fly.
Answer my questions when I ask why.

Teach me that failures are successes not tried.
Teach me to open my arms up wide.

Teach me to love and to laugh and to live.
Teach me to work and to share and to give.

Teach me so that I become all I can be.
Then stand back and be proud of me.

www.summerbridgeactivities.com   **Reading Connection—Grade 3—RBP3829**

Read and Think

1. Who is this poem written by and to?
   A. by a child, to a parent or teacher
   B. by a child, to a classmate
   C. by a teacher, to a student

2. What is this poem saying?
   A. Teach children to fly like birds.
   B. Teach children to be all they can be.
   C. Teach parents to smile a lot.

3. Read line 7. What does "failures are successes not tried" mean?
   A. You are successful when you fail.
   B. You don't need to try.
   C. You are a success if you try.

Try to Apply

1. Everybody gets mad sometimes. Put an **X** by the three things that are good to do when you are mad.
   _____ shout
   _____ talk about your feelings
   _____ call someone a name
   _____ take some time to calm down
   _____ take a deep breath
   _____ hit someone

Word Attack

1. Draw a line between the opposites.

laugh	get
love	happy
work	cry
give	rest
sad	hate

2. What do you think the phrase "open my arms up wide" means?

   _____

   _____

   _____

   _____

3. There are four types of sentences:
   A <u>statement</u> tells something and ends with a period.
   A <u>question</u> asks something and ends with a question mark.
   An <u>exclamation</u> says something with feeling and ends with an exclamation point.
   A <u>command</u> tells someone to do something and ends with a period.
   Each sentence in the poem is the same type. Read the poem. Write the type of sentence in the poem. _____

Rachel was walking out of the school building looking sad. Her mother was waiting for her. "Hey, why the long face?" her mother asked.

"Today was boring," replied Rachel. "There were no tests, nothing special for lunch, no extra recesses, no special programs. It was just an ordinary day."

"But it's the ordinary days that make the exciting days seem exciting. If we didn't have ordinary days, we would never notice the exciting days," Rachel's mother explained.

Rachel thought about what her mother had said. Maybe ordinary days were as special as exciting days.

Read and Think

1. Why was Rachel sad?
   - A. She got a bad grade on a test.
   - B. She had an argument with her friend.
   - C. She had an ordinary day.

2. What did Rachel learn?
   - A. that ordinary days make exciting days more exciting
   - B. occasionally everyone has a bad day
   - C. that her mother had a bad day, too

3. Carefully read the list below. In the space, put an exclamation mark for exciting or a period for ordinary. On the lines, write a sentence that would make things even more exciting.

   You get to have your party at Disneyland_____

   Your mom gives you a birthday party at home with cake and ice cream_____

   _____

   _____

   Your friends invite you to go swimming_____

   Your dad takes you swimming with the dolphins at Sea World_____

   _____

   _____

   You get to see your favorite singer in concert_____

   You get to watch your favorite singer on TV_____

   _____

   _____

Try to Apply

1. Number the following events in the order of how exciting they are to you. Make the most exciting number 1 and the least exciting number 6.

   _____ spelling test

   _____ hamburger at lunch

   _____ birthday party

   _____ special school program

   _____ library day

   _____ extra recess

Word Attack

1. What is the opposite of special?

   _____

2. What does the phrase "long face" mean?
   - A. sad look
   - B. happy look
   - C. excited look

Study Hall

1. Where should Rachel look to find exciting games to play at recess?

   _____ dictionary

   _____ newspaper

   _____ encyclopedia

   _____ a children's book about outside activities

Grandpa Remembers

1   My grandpa lives just down the lane and around the corner from my family. I love to go to his house and spend time with him. He taught me how to fish and play checkers. In the wintertime, we sit by the fire and play games. In the summertime, we go for long walks. Time always flies with my grandpa. My favorite times with Grandpa are the "remembering" times. Grandpa loves to tell stories about how things used to be. Grandpa always says he hopes he doesn't talk my ear off. But I love to listen to Grandpa's stories. Here's one of them.

2   "One nippy winter's day, when I wasn't much older than you," Grandpa began, "I begged to go with my dad to harvest a crop of ice blocks."

3   "A crop of ice blocks? You're pulling my leg, Grandpa," I interrupted.

4   "No interrupting," Grandpa would say. That was his rule—no interrupting.

5   "When I was young, my family didn't have refrigerators like we do now. Gathering ice blocks was the only way to keep foods cold through the spring and summer," Grandpa explained.

6   "I helped my dad get the tractor and wagon hooked up. Then down to the river we went. When we got there, Dad tested the ice. 'Looks like we found an excellent stretch of ice,' he'd say. Then he took out the logging saw. A logging saw is a long saw with handles at each end. I watched as my dad put the saw in the water. Pushing and then pulling, he cut a long slab of ice. Then I helped him move the slab up the bank to the wagon. He let me hold onto one end of the saw, and we worked together to cut the slab into square blocks. Then my dad used large ice tongs to put the blocks of ice on the wagon. When the ice blocks were loaded, we hit the road and headed to the ice shed. The ice shed had three or four inches of sawdust on the floor. We put the blocks on top of the sawdust. Then we packed more sawdust around the blocks. We would store all our ice cream and other foods that needed to stay cold inside the ice shed."

7   The "remembering" times were some of my favorite times with my grandpa. It was fun to shoot the breeze with him and learn about how things were when he was my age. I will always remember our "remembering" times. Someday it will be fun to have remembering times with my own grandchildren.

www.summerbridgeactivities.com   **Reading Connection—Grade 3—RBP3829**

Read and Think

1. What are "remembering" times?
   A. telling stories of long ago
   B. remembering what needs to be done
   C. listening and trying to remember details of a story

2. Number the sentences as they happened in Grandpa's story.
   _____ We put the blocks of ice in the ice shed.
   _____ We went down to the river.
   _____ He cut a slab of ice.
   _____ We loaded the blocks of ice on the wagon.
   _____ We worked together to cut the slab into square blocks.

3. How do you think the author of the story feels about his grandpa?
   A. loves him
   B. feels sorry for him
   C. thinks he's a bit crazy

4. Draw a line between each saying and its meaning.

   pulling my leg   talked too much

   hit the road   get going

   talked my ear off   talk about nothing in particular

   shoot the breeze   time passes quickly

   time flies   teasing me

Try to Apply

1. Write about a time you remember.
   _____
   _____
   _____
   _____

Word Attack

When a word ends with a vowel and a consonant, the consonant is usually doubled before adding **-ed** or **-ing**. Double the last consonant in the word in ( ). Then add -ing or -ed and write the word in the blank.

1. I _____ to go harvest a crop of ice. (beg)

2. A _____ saw has handles at each end. (log)

3. Grandpa was _____ a long slab of ice. (cut)

Words that tell about something are called **adjectives**. Circle the word the adjective tells about in the paragraph in ( ).

4. long (1)
   fish   wintertime   walks

5. remembering (1)
   stories   family   times

6. winter's (2)
   walk   day   nap

Bubble Fun

1　Kate and Nicole decided to wash the car. They gathered sponges, rags, and a bucket of soapy water. Kate put her sponge into the soapy water. She noticed bubbles coming from the bucket. They were large and clear. "Look at the bubbles!" Kate exclaimed. The bubbles gave Nicole an idea. She ran inside.

2　She came back with a bottle of corn syrup, a slotted spoon, and several wire coat hangers. Kate watched closely as Nicole poured the syrup into the soapy water. Then Nicole dipped the slotted spoon into the bucket. She waved the spoon around. Bubbles floated everywhere. Kate caught a bubble. She held it in her hand. It didn't pop. The corn syrup made the bubbles stronger. Then Nicole showed Kate how to bend a wire hanger into a bubble wand. The girls had so much fun, they forgot about washing the car.

3　Nicole's dad saw the fun the girls were having. He finished washing the car. Then he joined the girls for some bubble fun.

© RBP Books　　www.summerbridgeactivities.com　　Reading Connection—Grade 3—RBP3829

Read and Think

1. What is the main idea?
   A. how to wash a car
   B. having fun making bubbles
   C. dads always finishing what kids start

2. Number the sentences in the order they happened in the story.
   _____ Nicole poured corn syrup in the soapy water.
   _____ Dad joined the girls for some bubble fun.
   _____ Kate noticed the bubbles coming from the bucket.
   _____ The girls had fun making bubbles.
   _____ Nicole ran inside to get corn syrup, a slotted spoon, and wire coat hangers.

3. What did the girls gather to wash the car?
   A. corn syrup, a slotted spoon, and several wire coat hangers
   B. bubble wands
   C. sponges, rags, and a bucket of soapy water

4. Who finished washing the car?
   A. Kate and Nicole
   B. Nicole's dad
   C. only Nicole

5. What is a slotted spoon?
   A. a spoon used to blow bubbles
   B. a very large spoon
   C. a spoon with holes in it

Language Skills

Some words, like *I, she, he, we, they*, and *it*, are used in place of other words. They are called **pronouns**. Read each sentence. The pronoun is underlined. Look in the paragraph in ( ). Find the sentence. Find the noun the pronoun stands for. Circle the correct answer.

1. They gathered sponges, rags, and a bucket of soapy water. (1)
   Dad   Kate and Nicole   neighbors

2. They were large and clear. (1)
   sponges   buckets   bubbles

3. She waved the spoon around. (2)
   Kate   Mom   Nicole

4. She held it in her hand. (2)
   spoon   bucket   bubble

5. He finished washing the car. (3)
   Nicky   Dad   mechanic

Word Attack

An **antonym** is a word that means the opposite of another word. Read each word. Find the antonym in the paragraph in ( ). Write it in the blank.

1. little (1) _____

2. boys (3) _____

3. outside (1) _____

4. front (2) _____

5. weaker (2) _____

The Library

1   Jen was new in town. Her family had just moved from the country. Jen's new house was just down the street from the public library. Jen had never been to a public library. She had only been to the small library at her old school. But this library was a large, three-story building. From the outside, Jen thought it looked a bit scary.

2   However, Jen loved books so much that she got up enough courage to go inside the large building. As she walked in the door, Jen stopped. She looked all around. She had never seen so many books at one time. Jen felt a little overwhelmed. Marie, one of the librarians, noticed Jen standing frozen by the front door. She offered to show Jen around the library. Marie took Jen up the elevator to the third floor where the children's library was. Marie showed Jen how the books were shelved and how to locate her favorite authors. Then Marie showed Jen the computers that were used to locate books. At Jen's old school library, she used a card catalog to locate books. The computer made it much simpler. Jen spent hours looking through the books. Finally, Jen chose a mystery book to check out.

3   Jen took the book with her to the first floor. She walked to the checkout counter. Marie greeted her with a smile. She helped Jen fill out an application for a library card. Then she helped Jen check her book out. As Jen walked out of the library with her book in hand, she knew she had found a new favorite place.

    www.summerbridgeactivities.com   **Reading Connection—Grade 3—RBP3829**

Read and Think

1. What would be another good name for this story?
   A. The New Girl in Town
   B. Jen's First Visit to the Library
   C. The Nice Librarian

2. Why did Jen think the library looked a bit scary?
   A. The library was dirty and run-down.
   B. The library was far away from her house.
   C. The library was a large, three-story building.

3. Marie noticed Jen standing frozen. What does the word <u>frozen</u> mean in this sentence?
   A. not moving
   B. cold
   C. icy

4. How did Jen feel as she left the library?
   A. still a little scared
   B. tired from reading all those books
   C. happy because she had found a new favorite place

5. Write about a time that you felt a little overwhelmed by a new experience.

   _____

   _____

   _____

   _____

   _____

Study Hall

A **table of contents** can be found at the front of a book. It shows what chapters are in the book and on what page each chapter begins. Use the table of contents below to answer the questions.

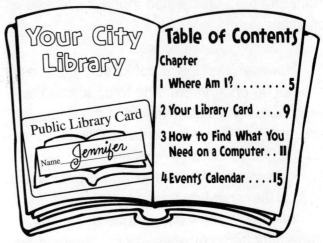

1. Which chapter would tell you if the library were open on Halloween? _____

2. What chapter might tell you how to replace your lost library card? _____

3. Which chapter would tell you where the library's mystery book section is? _____

4. On what page does the chapter on computers begin? _____

Language Skills

A **pronoun** is a word that takes the place of a noun. A pronoun is underlined in each sentence below. Read the paragraph in ( ). Find the sentence in that paragraph. Circle the word the pronoun stands for.

1. <u>She</u> looked all around. (2)   Marie   Jen

2. <u>She</u> helped Jen fill out an application. (3)
   Marie   Jen

3. She knew <u>she</u> had found a new favorite place. (3)   Marie   Jen

Mind Travel

1   My name's Eliot Mason Lucas Macoy,
    I'm nine and in third grade this year,
    And since the time I was a small boy,
    I've wandered the world far and near.

2   See, I love to travel to places for fun,
    But I'm small and, of course, I can't drive,
    And my mom took away my allowance;
    I was lucky to get out alive!

3   It's hard if you like to travel for fun,
    And your money is in short supply,
    So, some magic is something I wished for,
    And I'll bet you don't have to ask why.

4   My teacher says you can travel by book,
    Through a thing called imagination,
    Now, I'm going downtown with my library card,
    And the library's my destination.

5   I've checked out a book on geography,
    To learn about places to visit,
    Then when people tell me that Ireland's nice,
    I politely smile and say, "Is it?"

6   Well, I've traveled the ocean to Ireland's hills,
    I've seen shamrocks and leprechauns' gold,
    And surely I've read the Loch Ness monster is real,
    Or so is the tale I've been told.

7   It all happened because of my teacher's advice,
    Travel through imagination.
    Incredible trips begin with a book,
    It's a great way to start a vacation.

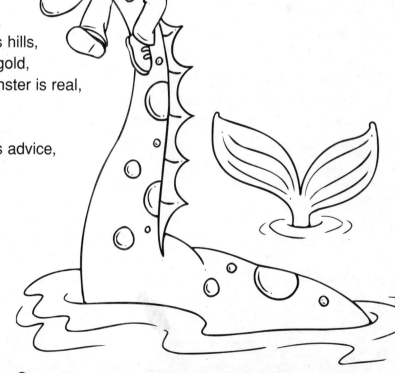

© RBP Books   www.summerbridgeactivities.com   Reading Connection—Grade 3—RBP3829

Read and Think

Circle the correct answer.

1. In verse 6, when Eliot says, "I've traveled the ocean to Ireland's hills," he really means _____.
   A. a ship took him to Ireland
   B. he rode his bike in the countryside
   C. he visited Ireland in his imagination

2. What was Eliot's teacher's advice?
   A. Eliot should stop traveling.
   B. She told him to go to the library and read books.
   C. Eliot should ride places in the Bookmobile.

3. List three reasons Eliot can't travel by himself.
   A. _____
   B. _____
   C. _____

4. In verse 2, Eliot's mom has taken his money. From what you read in the poem, write one reason you think he might have lost his allowance.
   _____
   _____
   _____

Word Attack

An 's at the end of a word is often used to show something belongs to a person or thing. Other times 's is used in a contraction to mean "is." Read each pair of sentences. Write **B** if the 's means "belongs to." Write **C** if the 's makes a contraction.

1. ____ My name's Eliot.
   ____ His name's first letter is E.

2. ____ Sam's leg was broken.
   ____ Sam's hard to catch.

3. ____ The books for children are on the library's third floor.
   ____ The library's my destination.

4. ____ I've traveled to Ireland's hills.
   ____ People tell me Ireland's nice.

Study Hall

1. Number these Irish cities in alphabetical order.
   ____ Dublin   ____ Londonderry
   ____ Limerick   ____ Dursey
   ____ Cork   ____ Belfast
   ____ Donegal   ____ Kilarney

2. A dictionary shows words divided into **syllables** by using a dot. Write the number of syllables for each word below on the line.
   ____ wan•dered   ____ tra•vel
   ____ i•ma•gi•na•tion   ____ li•brar•y
   ____ des•ti•na•tion   ____ ge•o•gra•phy
   ____ in•cre•di•ble   ____ va•ca•tion

The Food Guide Pyramid

The Food Guide Pyramid shows the groups of foods you should eat every day to be healthy. The pyramid shape gives a picture of the different amounts of each type of food that should be eaten. The foods at the bottom of the pyramid—breads, cereals, rice, and pasta—should make up most of the food eaten each day. Fats, oils, and sweets are at the top of the pyramid. Only small amounts of these should be eaten.

The bread, cereal, rice, and pasta group is a major source of energy. Six to eleven servings should be eaten each day. The more active you are, the more servings you need from this group. The fruit and vegetable group is next going up the pyramid. Three to five servings from the group are recommended. Fruits and vegetables provide important nutrients to make the body healthy. The milk and cheese group and the meats, eggs, and nuts group are next. Two to three servings of foods from these groups should be eaten each day. These groups provide protein to make the body strong. Milk and cheese provide calcium needed for strong bones and teeth. Finally, at the top of the pyramid is the fats, oils, and sweets group. Although some of these are necessary for a healthy body, they should be eaten in small amounts.

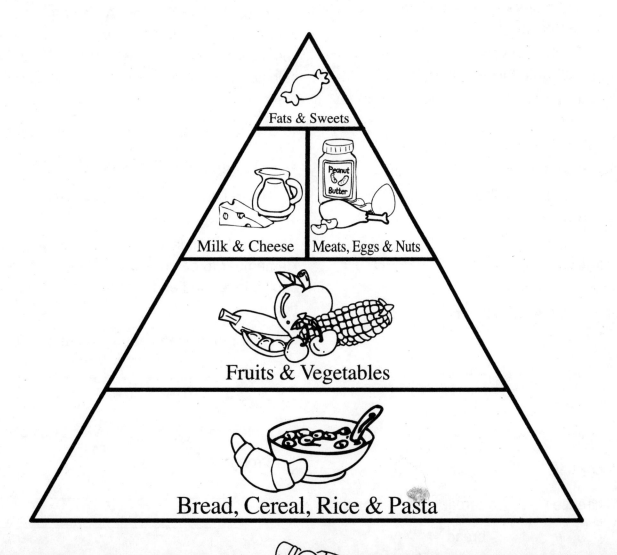

© RBP Books   www.summerbridgeactivities.com   Reading Connection—Grade 3—RBP3829

Read and Think

1. What is the Food Guide Pyramid?
   A. a list of food the Egyptians ate
   B. a guide for healthy eating
   C. a shopping list

2. Put a **T** by the sentences that are true. Put an **F** by the sentences that are false.
   _____ Foods at the bottom of the pyramid should be eaten only in small amounts.
   _____ Breads, cereals, rice, and pasta provide energy.
   _____ Don't ever eat any fats, oil, or sugar.
   _____ Eat one serving from each group to be healthy.
   _____ Fruits and vegetables provide important nutrients for the body.
   _____ Milk and cheese provide calcium for strong bones and teeth.

3. What does the word <u>nutrient</u> mean?
   A. things in foods that provide nutrition
   B. part of the nut family
   C. vitamins you get from eating certain fruits

4. Cross out the word that does not belong in each group.

   A. apple   orange   milk
      banana   pear

   B. meat   candy bar   nuts
      chicken   eggs

   C. cheese   cereal   pasta
      rice   bread

Try to Apply

1. Write your five favorite foods. Which food group does each food belong to?

   _____
   _____
   _____
   _____
   _____

Language Skills

A **main verb** is the most important verb in the sentence. It shows action. A **helping verb** works together with the main verb. Forms of the verbs *be* and *have* are helping verbs. Circle the helping verb in each sentence. Underline the main verb.

1. These are needed for a healthy body.

2. Only small amounts should be eaten.

3. These can make the body strong.

Write each sentence in the correct order. Remember to begin each sentence with a capital letter and end with the correct punctuation mark.

4. you of to all kinds need food healthy be

   _____
   _____

5. protein to body these provide the make strong

   _____
   _____

kidswilltravel.com

Web Site

1   Did you know that a bike was once called a *velocipede*? Most kids have a bike by the time they can walk. The idea of a bike came from a child's toy, the hobbyhorse. A hobbyhorse had a horse's head on one end of a stick and a wheel on the other.

2   The 1890s were called the "Golden Age of the Bicycle." But bicycles turned up long before then. Some people saw pictures of bikes on tomb walls in Egypt. One story says Leonardo da Vinci drew a picture of a modern-looking bicycle in 1490.

3   There have been many funny-looking bikes. At first, bikes had no pedals. People made them go by pushing with their feet, like a scooter. Then a blacksmith made the first pedals. Many of the bikes had a large front wheel that was turned by hand. People believed the large wheel would make the bike go faster. Most of the first bikes were made of wood and couldn't turn or stop.

4   Many new inventions helped make a better bicycle. The front tire was made to turn and help steer. Early bikes had solid tires that made the bicycle bounce and shake. People had a nickname for bikes. They called them "boneshakers." Then a man invented a new kind of tire. He put a hose on his son's trike and filled the hose with air. The man called it the pneumatic (new-ma-tick) tire. A rider used to have to jump off a bike to make it stop. Someone added brakes in 1898. Bikes also got lights, bells, and rearview mirrors.

5   Bikes were not as popular once people started driving cars. Then bike racing became a major sport. The Tour de France is the best example of bicycle racing. But it's okay if you aren't a racer. The bicycle is still a cheap way to travel for kids all over the world. And it is faster than walking!

© RBP Books   www.summerbridgeactivities.com   Reading Connection—Grade 3—RBP3829

Read and Think

Circle the correct answer.

1. The idea of a bike came from _____.
   A. a wheelbarrow
   B. a wagon wheel
   C. a child's toy

2. _____ were called the "Golden Age of the Bicycle."
   A. the teenage years
   B. the1890s
   C. summer days

3. A _____ made the first pedals.
   A. toy maker
   B. blacksmith
   C. carpenter

Word Attack

A **compound word** is two words put together to make one. Find the compound words in the story. Write them below.

1. _____
2. _____
3. _____
4. _____
5. _____
6. _____

An **antonym** is a word that means the opposite of another word. Find the antonym for each word listed. Look in the paragraph numbered in ( ).

7. begin (1) _____

8. worst (5) _____

9. sad (3) _____

10. start (4) _____

11. emptied (4) _____

12. few (3) _____

13. expensive (5) _____

14. no one (4) _____

Language Skills

Use one word from each column to write a true sentence about what you have read. Each sentence should be six or seven words long. Write two sentences.

Noun	Verb	Object
kids	invented	pedals
blacksmith	ride	picture
Leonardo da Vinci	drew	bikes

1. _____

   _____

   _____

2. _____

   _____

   _____

Reading Connection—Grade 3—RBP3829   www.summerbridgeactivities.com   ©RBP Books

Riding a bicycle can be fun. You get a sense of pride from learning to ride without training wheels. You also get a sense of freedom from riding your bike to explore new places. Unfortunately, every year children get hurt in bike accidents. It is important to learn and follow some bicycle safety rules.

First, make sure your bicycle is working properly. Check the brakes. Be sure that they stop the bike easily. The handlebars and the pedals should be tightly secure. If any part is not in good working order, fix it before riding your bike.

Next, check your safety equipment. Be sure that your bike has reflectors. Reflectors help drivers and other riders see you. Be sure to wear a bicycle helmet. Bicycle helmets will protect your

head if you fall off the bicycle. You should always wear shoes when riding a bike. Make sure your shoelaces are tied so they don't get tangled up with the pedals.

Once you have checked your bicycle and your safety equipment, you are ready to ride. Always ride your bike in the direction of traffic. Use bike paths whenever possible. Otherwise, stay close to the side of the road. Follow all traffic signs. Use arm signals to tell others you are changing directions. Pay attention. Be aware. Car drivers don't always pay attention to bicycle riders. So make sure you are aware of the dangers around.

Read and Think

1. What is the main idea?
   A. Wearing your helmet is important.
   B. Cars don't watch for bicycle riders.
   C. Follow the bicycle safety rules.

2. Put a **T** by the sentences that are true. Put an **F** by the sentences that are false.

   _____ If any of the parts of your bike need to be fixed, ride carefully.

   _____ Wear a helmet unless it is too uncomfortable.

   _____ Reflectors help drivers see you.

   _____ Always ride in the direction of traffic.

   _____ Use arm signals to tell others you are changing directions.

3. Why is it important to follow the bicycle safety rules?

   _____

   _____

   _____

Word Attack

1. Use the correct **homonym** in each sentence.

   A. Check the _____ on your bike.

      (brakes   breaks)

   B. Use common _____ when riding your bike.
      (cents   sense)

   C. Be sure the _____ on your bike are tight.
      (pedals   petals)

Language Skills

An **adverb** is a word that tells about a verb. Adverbs often end in *-ly*. Choose a word to fill in the blank. Add the correct ending to make it an adverb. One of the words needs one more change.

1. Make sure your bike is working _____.
   time   proper

2. Check to see if the brakes stop the bike _____.
   easy   hard

3. Don't follow _____ behind the rider ahead of you.
   high   close

Word Attack

A **compound word** is two words put together to make one word. Choose two words to make one and fill in the blank for each sentence.

1. A _____ is a bike that has an engine.

2. Don't let your _____ get tangled in the spokes.

3. Many bikes have the brakes on the _____.

   _____

4. The city park has a _____ if you want to see how fast your bike is.

Try to Apply

1. On a separate sheet of paper, make a poster about bicycle safety.

Life Is a Race: Travel Safely

Bicycle Safety Guidelines from Eisner Elementary School Safety Board

1. Always wear a helmet when you ride your bike. The helmet should have a snug fit and a strong strap and buckle.

2. Don't ride a bike that is too large for you. It may be hard to control. Make sure both feet can touch the ground when you are on the bike.

3. You should know how to stop the bike with the brakes. The brakes are usually on the handlebars. Some bikes use the pedals to brake.

4. Check your bike to make sure tires, brakes, and other mechanical parts are in good working order.

5. Make sure you have permission to ride in the street. Ride on the right side of the road in single file.

6. Don't wear loose clothes. They may catch in the chain or wheels, or on the pedals.

7. Observe traffic rules. Learn the correct hand signals for stopping and making turns.

8. Never ride with another person on your bike. It is hard enough to keep your balance and not fall.

9. Keep your hands and feet on the bike while riding.

10. Stay a safe distance behind other bike riders.

www.summerbridgeactivities.com   **Reading Connection—Grade 3—RBP3829**

Read and Think

Can you match the parts of the bike to the picture? Write the number of the part in the blank.

1. reflector
2. bell
3. pedals
4. chain
5. seat
6. spokes
7. handlebars
8. tires

Cause is why something happens. **Effect** is what takes place afterward. Read the rule number in ( ). Predict what might happen if you don't follow the rule.

9. (3) _____

_____.

10. (7) _____

_____

11. (9) _____

_____

Word Attack

Read each sentence. Circle the sentence if the underlined word means the same as the word in the rule number in ( ).

1. a. Marla <u>ground</u> (2) the meat for the hamburger patties.
   b. Make sure the apples don't fall to the <u>ground</u>. (2)
2. a. Afton wrote a <u>check</u> (4) for her groceries.
   b. I will go and <u>check</u> (4) to see if Simon is ready.
3. a. Walking is a <u>safe</u> (4) way to travel.
   b. The burglar broke into the <u>safe</u>. (4)
4. a. James thinks he is always <u>right</u> (5).
   b. Set the table with the knife on the <u>right</u> (5) side of the plate.
5. a. The queen <u>rules</u> (7) the country of England.
   b. I hope the new principal doesn't give us too many <u>rules</u>. (7)

Try to Apply

Think of something people do that might be dangerous. Write it in the blank. Then make a list of your own safety rules.

1. _____

A. _____

_____

B. _____

C. _____

Heroes

©RBP Books

1 Heroes are people like you and me,
   Who choose to act selflessly.

2 Heroes give all they have, then give some more.
   Heroes take action when action's called for.

3 Heroes pick themselves up when they make mistakes.
   Heroes keep trying. They've got what it takes.

4 Heroes are willing to give their all,
   They stop, look, and listen, then answer the call.

5 We look to heroes to show us the way,
   To go the extra mile, to seize the day.

6 So be kind and helpful wherever you go,
   For someone may look to you as a hero.

© RBP Books   www.summerbridgeactivities.com   Reading Connection—Grade 3—RBP3829

Read and Think

1. Put an **X** by the sentences that describe a hero.

   _____ Heroes choose to act selflessly.

   _____ Heroes give it their all.

   _____ Heroes make lots of money.

   _____ Heroes keep trying.

   _____ Heroes are very tall.

   _____ Heroes go the extra mile.

2. Why should you be kind and helpful?

   A. because someone may think you are a hero

   B. because your mom wants you to be

   C. because other people will be kind to you

3. Who is your hero? Write two things that make this person a hero.

   _____

   _____

   _____

4. "Heroes pick themselves up when they make mistakes" means what?

   A. They stand up when they fall down.

   B. They try again when they make a mistake.

   C. They always do things right.

5. "Give it their all," "Go the extra mile," and "Seize the day" are all sayings that mean what?

   A. be a good friend

   B. never give up

   C. believe in yourself

Word Attack

An **antonym** is a word that means the opposite of another word. Read the word. Find its antonym in the verse in ( ). Write the word in the blank.

1. take (2)   _____

2. go (4)   _____

3. night (5)   _____

4. none (4)   _____

5. question (4) _____

6. come (5)   _____

7. less (2)   _____

Language Skills

Read the sentence. Circle the subject, underline the verb, and put an **X** on the object.

1. Heroes make mistakes.

2. They answer the call.

3. Heroes seize the day.

4. We go the extra mile.

5. Heroes treat others kindly.

Heroes of Long Ago

1   Knights were heroes of long ago. They were soldiers in Europe from about 900 to 1500 A.D. Knights lived before the time of guns and gunpowder. They fought in hand-to-hand combat. Knights served their king. They had a set of rules, also called a <u>code of conduct</u>, to obey.

2   Knights wore heavy suits called armor. The armor weighed about 55 pounds. The armor protected the knight during battle. For a knight, the armor was a symbol that stood for honor, valor, and chivalry. Because of this, knights wore their armor proudly.

3   Armor was not only worn for battle but also for tournaments. Tournaments were festivals where the knights competed for fun. The joust was the main contest at the tournaments. During the joust a knight would use a long spear or lance to try to knock another knight off his horse. The knights who won the joust would receive money, land, or sometimes permission to marry a young maiden.

Read and Think

1. What is the main idea?
   A. Knights fought in battles.
   B. Knights were heroes a long time ago.
   C. Knights had a code of conduct.

2. Put a **T** by the sentences that are true. Put an **F** by the sentences that are false.

   _____ Knights used guns to fight battles.
   _____ Knights wore heavy suits called armor into battle.
   _____ A lance is a long spear.
   _____ The knight's armor weighed about 55 pounds.

3. What is a code of conduct?
   A. a secret language knights used
   B. a set of rules knights had to follow
   C. a contest in a tournament

4. What is a joust?
   A. the knight's suit of armor, which was a symbol of honor, valor, and chivalry
   B. the prize for winning the battle
   C. a contest at a tournament where two knights would battle with long spears

Word Attack

1. Circle the silent letter or letters in each word.

   A. knight   D. code
   B. know   E. rule
   C. knock   F. compete

Write the word from the paragraph in ( ) that fits each definition.

2. fight between people or armies (1) _____

3. to work or do things for (1) _____

4. a sign or emblem (2) _____

5. put on the body (3) _____

6. to bang on a door (3) _____

Language Skills

A **possessive pronoun** takes the place of a noun that shows belonging. Read each sentence. Write the correct possessive pronoun in the blank.

1. Knights were loyal servants of _____ king.

2. _____ suit of armor weighed 55 pounds.

3. During jousting a knight rode _____ horse.

4. The knight who won could ask a maiden for _____ hand in marriage.

5. We have _____ own code of honor in class.

6. One of _____ ancestors could have been a knight.

Reading Connection—Grade 3—RBP3829   www.summerbridgeactivities.com   ©RBP Books

Betsy Ross

Betsy Ross is known as an American hero. She did not fight in wars. She did not become President. She was simply a seamstress. But her contribution to our country is still remembered today. Betsy Ross made the first United States flag.

In her journal, Betsy Ross wrote about a meeting with George Washington in May of 1776. Betsy attended the same church as George

Washington. George Washington, who was a general at the time, asked Betsy to create a new flag for the new country that would soon earn its independence. In July 1776, the Declaration of Independence declared that the United States was independent from Britain. On June 14, 1777, the Congress decided that the flag Betsy Ross made would be the flag of the United States. The flag was to represent the unity of the 13 colonies as one country. The new flag was first flown over Fort Stanwix, New York, on August 3, 1777.

Today our flag has 50 stars representing the 50 states. The 13 stripes represent the 13 original colonies. Our flag represents the freedoms we enjoy. We continue to honor the flag and the freedom it represents by saying the Pledge of Allegiance and singing "The Star-Spangled Banner." We even have set aside June 14th as Flag Day to honor the flag.

©RBP Books   www.summerbridgeactivities.com   Reading Connection—Grade 3—RBP3829

Read and Think

1. What is Betsy Ross best remembered for?
   A. fighting in a war
   B. marrying the President
   C. making the first flag

2. How did Betsy Ross know George Washington?
   A. George Washington was the President.
   B. He was her brother.
   C. They went to the same church.

3. Circle the sentence that is true.
   A. The stars on the flag represent the 50 states, and the stripes represent the 13 colonies.
   B. The stars on the flag represent the 50 states, and the stripes represent the number of battles won to gain our independence.
   C. The stars on the flag represent the 50 heroes of the war, and the stripes represent the 13 colonies.

Word Attack

1. The prefix **uni-** means "one."
   A. What does the word <u>unity</u> mean?

   _____

   _____

   B. Write two other words that have the prefix <u>uni</u>.

   _____

   _____

Write each syllable of the words below in the blanks. Use a dictionary to help.

2. American   ____ ____ ____ ____
3. contribution   ____ ____ ____ ____
4. attended   ____ ____ ____
5. independence   ____ ____ ____ ____
6. representing   ____ ____ ____ ____
7. allegiance   ____ ____ ____

Study Hall

The **index** of a book is usually at the back. It lists the book's topics in alphabetical order. It also lists the page numbers on which to find each topic. Read the index; then answer the questions.

colonies, 5, 7–9, 22
flags, 10, 15, 18–20
heroes, 6, 28–30
holidays, 19, 25

1. On what pages could you find the names of the 13 colonies? _____

2. What pages might have information about the life of Betsy Ross? _____

3. On what pages could you find information on Flag Day? _____

Try to Apply

1. On a separate sheet of paper, create a new flag for the United States. Write about what your flag represents.

Reading Connection—Grade 3—RBP3829   www.summerbridgeactivities.com   ©RBP Books

Benjamin Franklin

Benjamin Franklin was born January 17, 1705. He was a printer, a statesman, and an inventor.

At the age of 17, Ben Franklin began working as a printer. He printed newspapers and books. He wrote many of the things he printed. In 1732, Franklin wrote and published Poor Richard's Almanac. He also printed all of the money for the state of Pennsylvania.

Ben Franklin worked hard to make his state of Pennsylvania a better place to be. He made improvements in the postal system and the police force. He established the first public library. He also helped start the first fire station after a fire destroyed much of the city of Philadelphia. He was elected delegate of Pennsylvania to the Second Continental Congress in 1775. In 1776 he helped write the Declaration of Independence.

Franklin was also an inventor. He was always thinking of ways to do things faster and better. In 1741 he invented a stove that would heat and stay at a certain temperature. He invented a type of glasses that he could use to help him read in his old age. He is probably best known for the important discoveries he made with electricity in 1752.

Benjamin Franklin died April 17, 1790, at the age of 84. More than 20,000 people attended his funeral. He was an American hero who is still remembered today.

Read and Think

1. What is the main idea?
   A. Ben Franklin is an American hero.
   B. Ben Franklin should have been President of the United States.
   C. Ben Franklin was a great inventor.

2. Put a √ by the things that are true about Benjamin Franklin.
   _____ He wrote books and newspaper articles.
   _____ He worked as a mail carrier.
   _____ He was the President of the United States.
   _____ He helped write the Declaration of Independence.
   _____ He discovered facts about electricity.

3. Number the events in the order they occurred in Ben Franklin's life.
   _____ He died at the age of 84.
   _____ He became delegate of Pennsylvania.
   _____ He worked as a printer.
   _____ He was born on January 17, 1705.
   _____ He made important discoveries about electricity.

Try to Apply

1. On another sheet of paper, write an obituary for Benjamin Franklin describing his life and his accomplishments.

Word Attack

The suffixes **-er** and **-or** mean "one who does." Add the correct suffix to each underlined word.

1. One who <u>invents</u> is called an

   _____.

2. One who <u>prints</u> is called a

   _____.

3. One who <u>writes</u> is called a

   _____.

4. One who <u>helps</u> is called a

   _____.

Language Skills

Words like *after, although, because, until,* and *while* can be used to combine two sentences. Circle one of the words to help combine two sentences into one. Write the new sentence.

1. He invented a type of glasses. He wanted to be able to read in his old age.
   because   after

   _____

   _____

2. He helped start the first fire station. A fire destroyed much of Philadelphia.
   after   while

   _____

   _____

3. He is still an American hero today. He died on April 17, 1790.
   although   while

   _____

   _____

Abraham Lincoln

Abraham Lincoln was the sixteenth President of the United States. He was born in Kentucky in 1809. In 1830 he moved to Illinois, where he eventually studied law. In 1834, he was elected to the state legislature, and he served in the legislature until 1842. Then, in 1846, Lincoln ran for the United States House of Representatives and won. In 1858, he ran for senator and lost, but two years later, Lincoln ran for President and won.

He was sworn in as President of the United States on March 4, 1861. At this time, the states that made up the country were divided. The northern states wanted to end slavery. The southern states wanted to keep their slaves. In April of 1862, the Civil War began. In 1863, Lincoln's Emancipation Proclamation declared freedom for all slaves. In that same year, Lincoln gave a speech called the Gettysburg Address. In this famous speech he called for the states to work together. Finally, on April 9, 1865, the Civil War ended. During his presidency, Lincoln had brought an end to slavery and brought the states together.

On April 14, 1865, while attending a play at Ford's Theater, Abraham Lincoln was shot to death by John Wilkes Booth. Lincoln was the first President to be assassinated. Vice President Andrew Johnson then became the seventeenth President of the United States.

Abraham Lincoln was a hero to many people. He worked hard to make the United States a better place. He led the life of an honest man and was nicknamed "Honest Abe."

www.summerbridgeactivities.com Reading Connection—Grade 3—RBP3829

Read and Think

1. Which sentence tells the main idea?
   A. Abraham Lincoln was born in Kentucky.
   B. Abraham Lincoln was a hero to many.
   C. Lincoln brought an end to slavery.

2. What war did Lincoln deal with during his presidency?
   A. Civil War
   B. War of Independence
   C. World War I

3. What does <u>assassinated</u> mean?
   A. killed
   B. honored
   C. against slavery

4. Complete the timeline by placing the letters of each event in Lincoln's life by the correct date.
   A. April 9, 1865, the Civil War ended.
   B. In 1809 Lincoln was born.
   C. In 1861 Lincoln became the sixteenth President of the United States.
   D. In 1830 he moved to Illinois.
   E. In 1834 he was elected to the Illinois State Legislature.
   F. In 1846 he was elected to the House of Representatives.
   G. On April 14, 1865, he was shot to death.

Word Attack

Draw a line between the syllables.

1. president

2. legislature

3. representative

4. Emancipation Proclamation

5. Gettysburg Address

Language Skills

Words that tell about something are called **adjectives**. Add the describing words to make the sentences below more interesting. Rewrite the sentences.

1. Slavery was a problem in the war.
   civil   major

   _____

   _____

2. The Address was a speech given by President Lincoln.
   famous   Gettysburg

   _____

   _____

3. Abe Lincoln united the country.
   honest   divided

   _____

   _____

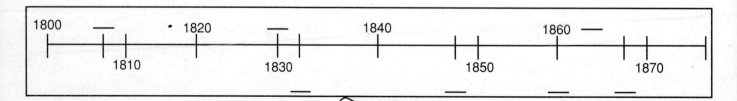

Martin Luther King, Jr.

Martin Luther King, Jr. was a hero who worked hard for racial equality. He was born on January 15, 1929.

Young Martin was a good student. His mother taught him to read before he started school. He skipped several grades and started college at age 15. After graduating from college he married Corretta Scott and became a minister.

In the 1950s, Martin joined the civil rights movement. This movement called for equality for African-Americans, and Martin led many peaceful demonstrations and spoke out against racism. In 1963, King gave his most famous speech, "I Have a Dream." In 1964, Congress passed the Civil Rights Act, which made segregation against the law. In 1964, Martin Luther King, Jr. was awarded the Nobel Peace Prize.

On April 4, 1968, while visiting Memphis, Tennessee, Martin Luther King, Jr. was shot to death. We celebrate the life of this American hero each year on the third Monday of January.

© RBP Books   www.summerbridgeactivities.com   Reading Connection—Grade 3—RBP3829

Read and Think

1. What is Martin Luther King, Jr. best remembered for?
   A. being a good student
   B. working hard for racial equality
   C. winning the Nobel Peace Prize

2. Number the sentences in the order they occurred in King's life.
   _____ King gave his "I Have a Dream" speech.
   _____ King was shot to death.
   _____ Martin Luther King was born on January 15, 1929.
   _____ Congress passed the Civil Rights Act.
   _____ Martin Luther King entered college at the age of 15.

Word Attack

1. Write the base word.

   graduation   _____

   celebration   _____

   demonstration _____

   segregation   _____

2. Draw a line from the word to its definition.

   graduate   to separate

   celebrate   to protest against

   demonstrate   to complete learning
                                        requirements

   segregate   to praise

Circle the correct meaning for the underlined word.

3. Martin skipped several grades at school.
   A. to leave something out or pass over
   B. to jump over
   C. to bounce forward, hopping on one foot

4. King joined the civil rights movement.
   A. to fasten two things together
   B. to come together with someone
   C. to become a member of a group

Try to Apply

1. Martin Luther King, Jr. gave a speech called "I Have a Dream." In this speech he spoke about his dream for people of all races to have equal rights and opportunities. What do you think would make the world a better place for all people?

   _____

   _____

Language Skills

Some verbs do not form the past tense by adding -ed. They change their form. These are called **irregular verbs**. Write the correct form of the verb in ( ).

1. Martin's mother _____ him how to read before he went to school. (teach)

2. The most famous speech he _____ was called "I Have a Dream." (give)

3. King was _____ in Memphis, Tennessee. (shoot)

4. Martin _____ at many civil rights demonstrations. (speak)

The Race of a Lifetime

Biography

1   No one knew it when Lance was born on September 18, 1971. His parents didn't know it when they gave him his first bike. But Lance knew that he would be a winner. He was a top swimmer and triathlete by age 13. Already, Lance Armstrong had started his race for life.

2   He began to train with the Junior National Cycling Team before he was out of high school. Then he joined the Motorola United States Cycling Team. They would compete all over the world. By 1996, he was the number one bike rider on earth. People expected him to win the Tour de France.

3   Instead, Lance found out he had cancer. It was spreading like wildfire. He had 11 tumors in his lungs. Some were as big as golf balls. He also had cancer in his brain and other parts of his body. Doctors told him he might not survive.

4   But Lance was a survivor. Lance had brain surgery and chemotherapy. He also believed that how people think could be helpful or harmful. He believed he would get well and began to train again after five months. In 1998, his cancer was behind him, and the Tour de France was ahead.

5   The first Tour de France began as a joke in 1903. Everyone loved it. By 2003, the race had been held 90 times. Many bike riders have finished the 2,077 miles. Each race is three weeks long. Some of the ride is on steep mountain roads. It's a great test of strength to get to the end.

6   In some of the first races, riders rode all day and night in the same clothes. Many riders threw broken glass and nails in the road where others were riding. Being a good sport has become more important since then. Lance Armstrong's bike flipped in the latest race. Another rider, Jan Ullrich from Germany, slowed down to give Lance a chance to get back on his bike. Jan showed he could play fair.

7   Lance got to wear his first yellow jersey in 1999. It was given to the winner of the Tour de France. In Paris, Lance said, "If you ever get a second chance in life, you've got to go all the way." He was on his way to five wins in a row. Lance Armstrong had traveled a long way from Texas to Paris.

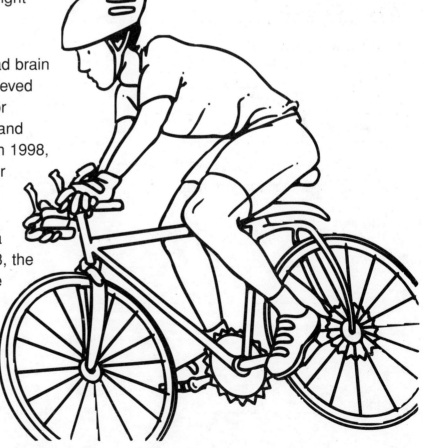

Read and Think

Fill out the timeline with the number that comes before each answer below. You can find the date each event happened by looking in the paragraph number listed in ( ).

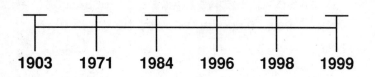

1903   1971   1984   1996   1998   1999

1. Lance Armstrong is born. (1)

2. Lance wins his first yellow jersey. (7)

3. The first Tour de France is held. (5)

4. Lance becomes the number one cyclist in the world. (2)

5. He was a top swimmer and athlete. (1)

6. His cancer was behind him. (4)

Word Attack

Write the **base word** for each of the words below. Use your dictionary to help.

1. winner _____

2. swimmer _____

3. triathlete _____

4. expected _____

5. survivor _____

6. riding _____

Language Skills

Words that tell about something are called **adjectives**. Find a word or phrase in the paragraph in ( ) that describes. List the words below.

1. _____ (7)

2. _____ (5)

3. _____ (6)

4. _____ (1)

Try to Apply

Lance Armstrong is a hero for many cancer survivors. Think of a person you know who could be your hero. Write three complete sentences that tell about your hero.

1. _____
   _____

2. _____
   _____

3. _____
   _____

Reading Connection—Grade 3—RBP3829   www.summerbridgeactivities.com   © RBP Books

Neighborhood Heroes

Life was pretty dull around our quiet neighborhood, so a couple of friends and I decided to become neighborhood news reporters. We thought that maybe if we looked for news, we'd find it. We used my tree house for our headquarters. Then we set up our headquarters with pencils, notebooks, clipboards, binoculars, and even a laptop computer and a cell phone. We began discussing topics we might want to report on. Max was looking through the binoculars. "Looks like we might have our first story," he said. "Georgie Willows is sitting on his front steps crying. You guys keep talking. I'll go see what's wrong with Georgie."

Soon Max was back. He wanted us to help him. "Georgie's hamster got loose in his yard. He can't find it anywhere." We all left the tree house and went to help. We looked everywhere. Suddenly we heard the dog next door barking. We went to investigate. Sure enough, the neighbor's dog had Georgie's hamster cornered in the garage. We rescued the frightened hamster and took him back to Georgie.

We went back to the tree house. This time I was looking over the neighborhood with the binoculars. As I looked over into Mrs. Stevens's backyard I saw her lying by her garden, clutching her chest. "Someone call 911. I think Mrs. Stevens is in trouble!" I yelled. Max called 911 while the rest of us ran to Mrs. Stevens. Mrs. Stevens wasn't moving. Last summer I had taken a first aid class and learned CPR. I started CPR on Mrs. Stevens. Soon the ambulance arrived, and the paramedics took over the CPR. They were able to revive Mrs. Stevens. They took her to the hospital. Mrs. Stevens had had a heart attack. Our quick thinking saved Mrs. Stevens's life. The local newspaper wrote an article about what happened. Now, instead of being the neighborhood reporters, we are known as the neighborhood heroes.

© RBP Books   www.summerbridgeactivities.com   Reading Connection—Grade 3—RBP3829

Read and Think

1. The poem on page 27 says, "Heroes take action when action's called for." What action did the neighborhood heroes take?

   _____

   _____

2. Why did the friends become neighborhood news reporters?

   A. because they were bored

   B. to get some writing experience

   C. because they liked news

3. Why did the friends call 911 when they saw Mrs. Stevens, but not when they saw Georgie?

   _____

   _____

   _____

Word Attack

A **synonym** is a word that means the same as another word. An **antonym** is a word that means the opposite. Write whether each pair of words are synonyms or antonyms.

1. dull   boring   _____

2. quiet   loud   _____

3. rescued   saved   _____

4. frightened   courageous   _____

5. exciting   dull   _____

6. scared   frightened   _____

Try to Apply

1. Write about a time when you helped someone.

   _____

   _____

   _____

   _____

   _____

Language Skills

The verb **be** tells what the subject of a sentence is or was. Examples of the verb *be* in the present are *am, is,* and *are*. Examples of the verb *be* in the past are *was* and *were*. Read each sentence. Write the correct verb in the blank.

am	is	are
was	were	

1. Max's quiet neighborhood _____ pretty boring. (past)

2. Where _____ Georgie Willows sitting? (present)

3. The two friends _____ neighborhood heroes. (present)

4. The dog and hamster _____ in the garage. (past)

5. Mrs. Stevens said, "I _____ glad those boys found me." (present)

Stray Cat Hero

My mom is always taking in stray animals. The one I remember best was a mangy-looking kitten.

One day a dirty, hungry little kitten wandered up on our porch. Mom took pity on the poor little thing. She brought it in the house, gave it a bath, and cleaned it up. She took special care of this kitten.

One night, we were all sound asleep. Around two in the morning, I heard this loud meowing. Mom's stray kitten jumped up next to my face and began to lick me. I pushed the cat away, rolled over, and went back to sleep. The persistent cat wouldn't take no for an answer. He went to my dad. My dad pushed the cat over to my mom's side of the bed. Although my mom is a very heavy sleeper, the cat continued to meow and lick her face. Finally, my mom woke up. At first she was annoyed. But then she realized what the cat wanted. Mom smelled gas. She immediately woke up Dad. They turned the gas off and opened all the windows. We had a gas leak that no one smelled except our stray cat.

We could have died from the gas, or our house could have exploded! Mom's stray cat had saved us. That's how the little stray kitten became our family pet, and that's how our cat, Hero, got his name!

www.summerbridgeactivities.com Reading Connection—Grade 3—RBP3829

Read and Think

1. Write a headline for this story.

_____

_____

2. Number the sentences in the order they
   happened in the story.

   _____ Mom took care of a stray cat.

   _____ We named the stray cat Hero.

   _____ The cat tried to wake up Dad.

   _____ The cat woke up Mom.

   _____ Mom smelled gas.

   _____ Mom and Dad turned off the gas.

Cause is why something happens. **Effect** is
what takes place afterward. Circle the correct
answer.

3. Because Hero woke up Mom
   A. she got scratched.
   B. she smelled the gas.
   C. they all woke up.

4. They opened all the windows
   A. to let Hero outside.
   B. because they were hot.
   C. because there was a gas smell.

5. Mom gave the kitten a bath
   A. because no one else would.
   B. because it was a stray.
   C. because it was dirty and she felt sorry
      for it.

Word Attack

Draw a line between the present tense and
past tense of each word.

1. take   brought

2. become   went

3. bring   began

4. begin   took

5. go   became

6. What is a stray animal?
   A. a wild animal
   B. a dirty, hungry animal
   C. an animal without a home

7. Someone who is <u>persistent</u> _____.
   A. doesn't give up
   B. is very loud
   C. can smell very well

Language Skills

Some sentences can be combined using the
word **and**. Use the word *and* to combine the
sentences below. Rewrite them in the space
below.

1. Our cat smelled smoke. He tried to wake us.

   _____

   _____

2. Mom takes in stray animals. She gives them
   a bath.

   _____

   _____

3. The cat tried to wake up Mom and Dad. The
   cat tried to wake me up.

   _____

   _____

Animal Poem

How many animals can you name?
This seems like a never-ending game.

There are little ants so very small.
There are spotted giraffes so very tall.

There are mammals and insects to name a few.
There are reptiles and amphibians in the zoo.

There are animals that fly and some that walk.
There are cows in a herd and birds in a flock.

There are animals that live on land and some that live at sea.
There are animals that live in the ground and some that live in trees.

There are animals that are wild and some that are tame.
There are just too many animals for us to ever name.

www.summerbridgeactivities.com   **Reading Connection—Grade 3—RBP3829**

Read and Think

1. What is the main idea of the poem?
   A. There are too many animals to name.
   B. Animals make great pets.
   C. Some animals are wild, and some are tame.

2. Three animals that are mentioned by name in the poem are
   A. giraffes, ants, and cows.
   B. sea animals, cows, and ants.
   C. sea turtles, crows, and ants.

Word Attack

1. Draw a line between the opposites.

   land   tame

   ground   sky

   wild   tall

   few   sea

   small   many

2. Find five nouns that are plural in the poem. Write them on the lines.

   _____

   _____

   _____

Try to Apply

Cross out the animal that does not fit in each group.

1. hawk   owl   whale   robin

2. horse   cow   sheep   giraffe

3. squirrel   monkey   dog   koala

4. snake   ants   cricket   grasshopper

5. tiger   lion   rabbit   leopard

6. See how many different animal names you can write in one minute.

Language Skills

You can make a sentence that ends with a period into a question. You can also make a question into a statement. Rewrite the sentences below to make statements into questions and questions into statements.

1. This seems like a never-ending game.

   _____

   _____

2. There are animals that fly and some that walk.

   _____

   _____

3. How many animals can you name?

   _____

   _____

Animals' Sleeping Habits

Sleep for humans almost always means a bed or a mat. Animals, however, have many different ways of sleeping.

For warmth, some animals sleep in groups. Lions, monkeys, and penguins are a few animals that sleep in groups. Elephants also sleep in a group, but they sleep in groups for protection. The larger elephants make a circle around the young elephants. The larger elephants sleep standing up, while the younger ones get inside the circle and lie down to sleep.

Some animals sleep in trees. Birds will lock their feet onto a branch to keep from falling out of the tree. Other animals, like squirrels and baboons, make nests in trees to sleep in. They curl up to keep warm. Bats hang upside down from tree branches to sleep.

Most animals look for warm, dry places to sleep. However, ducks often sleep in the water. Sea otters sleep in water, too. They float on their backs in the seaweed.

Most animals lie down to sleep. However, some large animals, like horses, sleep standing up. The flamingo sleeps standing on just one leg.

Most animals sleep at night, but some animals are nocturnal. Nocturnal animals sleep during the day. Bats are nocturnal animals. They wake up when the sun goes down.

Animals sleep in many different places and in many different ways. Still, just like humans, every animal must sleep.

Read and Think

1. Circle the sentence that tells the main idea.
   A. Sleep for humans almost always means a bed or a mat.
   B. Animals have many different ways of sleeping.
   C. Most animals sleep at night.

2. Put a **T** by the sentences that are true. Put an **F** by the sentences that are false.
   _____ All animals sleep at night.
   _____ Elephants sleep in groups for protection.
   _____ Birds are the only animals that build nests.
   _____ All animals sleep.

3. Draw a line from the animal to the way it sleeps.

elephant	standing on one foot
otter	in nests in trees
bat	upside down
flamingo	floating on its back
squirrel	in groups

Word Attack

1. What do nocturnal animals do?
   A. sleep in groups
   B. sleep at night
   C. sleep during the day

Language Skills

An **'s** is used at the end of a word to show that something belongs to a person or thing. (An ['] is added to the end of a plural word ending in *s*.) Read each sentence. Put an (') before or after the *s* in the underlined word to make the sentence correct.

1. The <u>elephants</u> circle protects the young elephants.
2. <u>Birds</u> feet lock to hold onto a branch.
3. That baby sea <u>otters</u> bed is a real water bed.
4. A <u>bats</u> bedtime is when my alarm clock rings to wake me up for school.

Study Hall

Topics in an encyclopedia are in **alphabetical order**. Write the number of the volume in which you would find each topic.

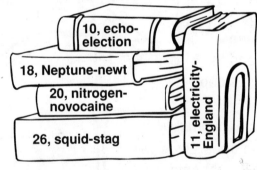

1. nocturnal _____
2. Einstein _____
3. elephants _____
4. squirrels _____

Try to Apply

1. Describe your sleeping habits.

_____

_____

_____

Reading Connection—Grade 3—RBP3829   www.summerbridgeactivities.com   ©RBP Books

Birds

1   Birds are unique animals. Birds have wings, feathers, and beaks. Birds are the only animals that have feathers. These feathers enable most birds to fly. Their ability to fly helps them stay alive because they can hunt for food, escape their enemies, and migrate away from bad weather. Feathers also protect a bird from getting too hot or too cold. Birds have beaks, but they do not have teeth. They use their beaks to get food. Birds eat insects, worms, seeds, and grains.

2   Birds are protective parents. Birds lay eggs. They build nests to protect their eggs. Usually the mother bird sits on the nest to keep the eggs warm. Both the mother and father bird keep watch over the nest before the eggs hatch. The nests continue to keep the baby birds warm after they hatch from their eggs. The adult birds take care of the baby birds until they are ready to fly. The parents bring food to the baby birds in the nest. The adult birds teach their babies how to fly and find food until one day the baby birds can fly off on their own.

Read and Think

1. Circle the sentence that tells the main idea.
   A. Birds are unique animals.
   B. The adult bird teaches its babies how to fly, find food, and build nests.
   C. Birds are one of the few animals that lay eggs.

Fill in the blanks with the correct answer.

2. Birds are the only animals that have

   _____.

3. Birds do not have _____.

4. Birds lay _____.

5. Birds build_____to protect their eggs.

6. Number the sentences in the order that they happen.
   _____ The parent brings food to the baby birds in the nest.
   _____ The mother bird sits on the nest to keep the eggs warm.
   _____ Birds build a nest to protect their eggs.
   _____ The adult birds teach their babies how to fly and find food.

7. Put a **T** if the sentence is true. Put an **F** if the sentence is false.
   _____ All birds can fly.
   _____ Flying helps birds find food.
   _____ Flying protects birds from their enemies.
   _____ Birds migrate to stay away from their enemies.
   _____ Some birds have large teeth.

Word Attack

1. What does <u>migrate</u> mean?
   A. to hide under trees
   B. to fly to other places
   C. to find shelter

Write the word in the paragraph in ( ) that can have the meaning below.

2. A flap on pants covering a zipper. (2)

   _____

3. A small clock worn on the wrist. (2)

   _____

4. To possess something. (2)_____

Language Skills

Action verbs tell what the subject of the sentence does. Circle the action verb in each sentence.

1. Birds fly using their feathers to help.

2. Birds eat with their beaks instead of teeth.

3. They build nests to protect their eggs.

4. The babies hatch from eggs.

5. The parents teach the baby birds how to fly.

The Ostrich

The ostrich is probably the most unique of all birds. The ostrich is the largest bird. It can grow to be eight feet tall and can weigh more than 200 pounds. Unlike most other birds, the ostrich cannot fly. Its long legs help it run very fast. It runs with its wings outstretched. It uses its strong legs to protect itself, and the ostrich will run or kick if it is threatened. The ostrich has no teeth.

The ostrich lays eggs and has feathers like other birds. Its eggs are extremely large. In fact, its eggs are almost the size of a football and can weigh nearly three pounds. The male ostrich digs a hole in the ground for the nest. The female ostrich lays her eggs in the hole. Then both parents protect the eggs until the chicks hatch. Often the female will sit on the eggs during the day, and the male will sit on the eggs during the night. After the chicks hatch, the parents continue to be very protective until the chicks can take care of themselves.

Read and Think

1. Circle the sentence that tells the main idea.
   A. The ostrich is the largest bird.
   B. The ostrich is probably the most unique bird.
   C. The ostrich lays eggs and has feathers like other birds.

2. Put a **T** if the sentence is true. Put an **F** if the sentence is false.

   ____ The ostrich has a lot of teeth.

   ____ The ostrich can run very fast.

   ____ The mother ostrich lays its eggs in a hole in the ground.

   ____ Most chicks leave their parents as soon as they are born.

   ____ The ostrich cannot kick without falling down.

3. Compare the ostrich to other birds. Put an **X** in the box that shows whether the characteristic describes the ostrich, other birds, or both.

	ostrich	other birds
cannot fly		
has feathers		
lays eggs		
grows to be 8 feet tall		
protective of its young		

Word Attack

Complete each sentence using the correct **homonym**.

1. The ostrich can grow to be _____ feet tall.
   (ate   eight)

2. The ostrich can weigh more than _____ hundred pounds.
   (too   two)

3. The ostrich egg can _____ nearly three pounds.
   (way   weigh)

4. The _____ ostrich digs a hole in the ground for the nest.
   (mail   male)

5. What does <u>unique</u> mean?
   A. one large bird
   B. having one feather
   C. one of a kind

The ending **-er** sometimes means "more." It may be used to compare two things. The ending **-est** means "most." It is used to compare more than two things. Write -er or -est in the blank.

6. The ostrich is large _____ than most birds.

7. It is probably the tall _____ of all birds.

8. Ostrich eggs are the large _____ eggs in the world.

9. Its powerful legs make it the fast _____ bird on the ground.

Seahorses are interesting sea animals. Seahorses swim upright. Fins on the sides of their bodies help them steer while they swim slowly through the water. Seahorses hide themselves among the seaweed. A small mouth, located at the end of the seahorse's snout, sucks up tiny fish.

One of the most interesting things about seahorses is their family life. The male seahorse gives birth to the young. The female seahorse deposits about one hundred eggs in the male's pouch. Each egg attaches itself inside the pouch. The female will visit the male seahorse every morning until the babies are born. It takes about 21 days for the baby seahorses to develop. The male seahorse then gives birth to the babies. Newborn seahorses are able to swim. They can eat sea plants, and they are left on their own to survive.

A couple of days after the birth of the babies, the male will join the female again. Within hours the female will deposit eggs in the male's pouch, and the life cycle of the seahorse continues.

Read and Think

1. Circle the sentence in the reading that tells the main idea.

Use the following words to complete the sentences.

male   **female**   **egg**

pouch   **mouth**

2. Each _____ attaches itself inside the pouch.

3. The seahorse uses its _____ to suck up tiny fish.

4. The _____ seahorse gives birth to the young.

5. The _____ seahorse deposits the eggs in the male's _____.

6. Draw a line through the sentence that is not true.

    A. Seahorses swim quickly through the water.

    B. The female deposits about one hundred eggs in the male's pouch.

    C. A seahorse's mouth is located at the end of its snout.

    D. Newborn seahorses take care of themselves.

    E. It takes three weeks for the baby seahorses to develop.

Word Attack

1. Circle the correct way to show more than one.

    A.   seahorse   seahorses   seahorsies

    B.   fin   fines   fins

    C.   baby   babies   babys

    D.   pouch   pouchs   pouches

    E.   body   bodys   bodies

2. Write the two little words that make up each compound word.

    A. seahorse   _____   _____

    B. upright   _____   _____

    C. seaweed   _____   _____

    D. newborn   _____   _____

    E. within   _____   _____

Study Hall

Guidewords are two words at the top of each page in the dictionary. The first guideword is the first defined word on the page. The second is the last word defined on the page. Write an **X** on the line if the word falls on the page with the two guidewords.

seasons–starfish

1. seahorse _____   snout _____

    stuck _____   seaweed _____

ear–elephant

2. each _____   deposits _____

    egg _____   every _____

Mammals

Mammals come in many shapes and sizes. They can be very large, like the elephant or the whale. They can be very small like the mouse. Mammals can fly in the sky, swim in the water, or walk on the ground. Mammals are different in many ways, but all mammals have a few things in common. All mammals have a backbone. Mammals are the only animals that have hair. All mammals breathe air. Even the dolphin, which spends most of its time in the water, must come to the surface to breathe air. All mammals are warm-blooded. A mammal's body temperature stays pretty much the same regardless of the outside temperature. Most mammals have babies that are born alive instead of hatching from eggs. All mammals feed their young milk until they are old enough to get food on their own.

Some mammals eat meat. Meat-eating mammals are called <u>carnivores</u>. Lions, dogs, and killer whales are carnivores. Some mammals eat only plants. These mammals are called <u>herbivores</u>. Horses, koalas, and beavers are herbivores. Other mammals, such as humans, eat both plants and meat. Mammals that eat meat and plants are called <u>omnivores</u>. Still other mammals eat only insects. These mammals are called <u>insectivores</u>. Insectivores include the aardvark and the anteater.

www.summerbridgeactivities.com   Reading Connection—Grade 3—RBP3829

Read and Think

1. Cross out the sentence that is not true about mammals.

    A. All mammals have a backbone.

    B. All mammals breathe air.

    C. All mammals are cold-blooded.

    D. All mammals feed their young milk.

2. Put an **M** if the animal is a mammal. Put an **N** if the animal is not a mammal.

    _____ cat

    _____ tiger

    _____ octopus

    _____ fish

    _____ owl

    _____ giraffe

    _____ robin

    _____ alligator

    _____ leopard

Mind Buster

Make a chart. Divide the chart into 5 columns and 5 rows down the side. List 5 different animals you like. They do not all have to be mammals. Across the top, list different qualities mammals have. Also list characteristics other kinds of animals have. Some examples are fur, breathe air, four legs, and lay eggs. Read about each of your animals. If the animal has the characteristic, mark an **X**. Now you can compare your favorite animals.

Word Attack

1. What does <u>warm-blooded</u> mean?

    _____

Place the correct word in each sentence.

carnivores   **herbivores**

omnivores   **insectivores**

2. Animals called _____ eat both plants and animals.

3. Animals that eat only meat are called

    _____ .

4. Animals that eat insects are called

    _____ .

5. Animals that eat only plants are called

    _____ .

Find words in the reading that have a long vowel sound. Put each word in the correct group.

6. long <u>a</u> spelled <u>a</u> consonant <u>e</u>

    _____

    _____

    _____

7. long <u>a</u> spelled <u>ay</u>

    _____

    _____

8. long <u>i</u> spelled <u>i</u> consonant <u>e</u>

    _____

    _____

    _____

9. long <u>i</u> spelled <u>y</u>

    _____

Driver Ants: All for One

Encyclopedia Article

1   Ants can be found almost anywhere on earth. Over 8,000 different kinds have been discovered. One thing is the same for all ants: They have always been ants.

2   Ants look the same today as they did when there were dinosaurs. That was 235 million years ago. Scientists found some ants from that time frozen in amber. Amber is tree sap, a sticky, gooey liquid. It hardened with the ants stuck inside. The ants looked like ants do now.

3   Most ants live in colonies. A colony has one very large queen, and she lays all the eggs. Most of the ants are females, but they don't lay eggs. The males die after mating with the queen.

4   The most fearsome ant of all lives in Africa. It is called the driver ant. There can be over 20 million driver ants in one colony.

5   Every single ant in the colony has a special job. There are the soldier ants that are larger than the worker ants. The soldiers have large mandibles that are like very sharp teeth. Their job is to protect the queen and the workers. But soldier ants can't feed themselves because of their teeth. It is the job of worker ants to get food to feed the queen and the soldier ants.

6   Driver ants eat meat. They are carnivorous. They will eat anything that cannot get away. Sometimes they eat large animals like cows. However, most of the time driver ants eat frogs, spiders, and insects like the cockroach and praying mantis. These ants can capture more than 100,000 insects a day.

7   People in the jungle move out of their huts and village when they hear driver ants are on the move. After the ants are gone, they come back to a village that is free from insects.

8   Driver ants are nomads. They eat and then move on to find more food. The ants travel from place to place and make no permanent home. If the queen is laying eggs, the colony stops for a while. They make a nest out of themselves. Some of them form walls, and others form the ceiling. When the babies, which are called grubs, can travel, the colony moves on.

9   Nothing stops driver ants on the move. These ants work very well as a team. They can build a bridge by climbing and hooking onto each other until they reach the other side of a stream. The African driver ant has been known to form a ball and float a whole colony on water. What great cooperation!

www.summerbridgeactivities.com   Reading Connection—Grade 3—RBP3829

Read and Think

Circle the correct answer.

1. The main idea of this article is _____.
   A. driver ants like to eat cows.
   B. ants can be found all over the world.
   C. driver ants are remarkable ants.

Facts and details tell more about a main idea.
Write the fact or detail in the blank.

2. The most fearsome ant is the_____.

3. Driver ants eat _____, _____,
   and _____.

4. The three special jobs of the driver ants are
   _____, _____, and
   _____.

5. Number the sentences in the order they
   happened.
   _____The grubs can travel.
   _____The queen is laying eggs.
   _____The ants make a nest out of
        themselves.
   _____They move on to find more food.

Cause is why something happens. **Effect** is
what happens afterward. Circle the correct
effect for each cause.

6. When driver ants are on the move,
   A. they hum as they go.
   B. people move out of their way.
   C. the queen lays eggs.

Language Skills

Write **C** if the sentence is complete. Write **I** if
the sentence is incomplete.

1. ____ Over 8,000 different kinds.
2. ____ Ants are found almost anywhere on
       earth.
3. ____ With the ants stuck inside.
4. ____ After the ants are.
5. ____ Driver ants are nomads.
6. ____ These ants work very well as a team.

Study Hall

Topics in an encyclopedia are in alphabetical
order. Write the number of the volume listed
below in which you would find each topic.

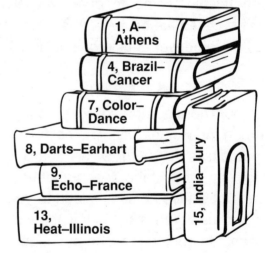

1, A–Athens
4, Brazil–Cancer
7, Color–Dance
8, Darts–Earhart
9, Echo–France
13, Heat–Illinois
15, India–Jury

1. dinosaurs _____

2. ants _____

3. jungle _____

4. insects _____

5. Africa _____

Why Worm Lives Underground

Nigerian Folktale

There was a time when Eyo III was ruler over all in the land. The great lord held a feast deep in the jungle at the House of Talk. Man and beast came to make speeches, eat, and drink.

When all had eaten much and drunk from the big bowl of *tombo*, the talk began. First to go to the palaver stand was High and Mighty, the driver ant. The palaver stand was where the great lord and his subjects went to speak. All parted way and made a path. So tiny was High and Mighty that many moved away so she was not flattened by a stray foot.

After many moments, the head driver ant reached the stand. Thousands of her workers climbed upon each other to make a tower.

When she reached the top of the stand, High and Mighty's voice echoed loud and deep. She told Eyo III and his subjects of the great driver ant clan. No one could match her people. They always got what they deserved and deserved what they got. The legend of their cooperation had spread far and wide. Even mighty Elephant's thunder was no match for the driver ants on the move.

High and Mighty was very proud. She said lowly Worm was lower than all the animals. It was for a simple reason. Worm could only wriggle. What a poor creature!

Worm and his tribe did not like such prideful talk. They begged King Eyo to arrange a contest. The Ant Clan would war against the Worm Tribe. It was to be a battle to the finish.

Of course, when all was over, it was no true match. Worm and the few of his tribe who remained inched away. They tunneled through the earth far from the battle scene. There they have remained to this day.

© RBP Books www.summerbridgeactivities.com

Read and Think

If something could really happen, it is **real**. Something that could not happen in real life is **make-believe**.

1. Circle the one that could not really happen.
   A. Man and beast came to make speeches.
   B. Worm could only wriggle.
   C. They tunneled into the earth.

2. The two main characters in this folktale are _____.
   A. Eyo III and Worm
   B. High and Mighty and Worm
   C. Eyo III and High and Mighty

3. Worm lives underground because _____.
   A. the rent is cheaper
   B. it is safe
   C. there is more food there

4. Number the sentences in the order they happened.
   _____ High and Mighty's voice echoed loud and deep.
   _____ The great lord held a feast.
   _____ It was a battle to the finish.

Word Attack

Write the correct **homonym** in the blank to complete each sentence.

1. They had to make a tower to reach the _____ stand.
   hi   high

2. The head driver ant _____ a speech.
   made   maid

3. _____ creature could survive the ants on the move.
   Know   No

4. The worms tunneled far from the battle _____.
   seen   scene

Language Skills

A **pronoun** is a word that stands for another. Read each sentence. Fill in the blank.

1. The head driver ant reached the stand. Thousands of her workers made a tower.
   Her stands for _____.

2. Worm and the few who survived inched away. They tunneled into the earth.
   They stands for _____.

3. An **adjective** is a word that describes something. Write three adjectives that describe High and Mighty. Write three adjectives about Worm. Choose words from those listed.

first	deserving	
lowly	prideful	cooperative
wriggly	tiny	poor

   High and Mighty   Worm

   1. _____   1. _____

   2. _____   2. _____

   3. _____   3. _____

I have a dog named Hollywood. Little did I know when I named my dog how fitting his name would be. Before his second birthday, my dog, Hollywood, made it to Hollywood!

Hollywood is a great dog, but he has a peculiar habit. Every day Hollywood barks at the mail truck. Many dogs bark at cars. But Hollywood only barks at the mail truck. One day, as the mail truck came down the street, Hollywood got out of the yard. He ran beside the mail truck and jumped in the open door while the truck was moving! Our mail carrier didn't even notice Hollywood. Then, at the end of the street, Hollywood jumped out and came back home. The next day, the same thing happened. This became a habit for Hollywood. Luckily our mail carrier likes dogs and enjoyed Hollywood's new trick. The newspaper put a picture of Hollywood on the front page and printed an article about Hollywood's peculiar habit.

A few days later, a dog trainer called. He said that he saw the article in the paper about Hollywood. He said he needed a dog like Hollywood for a new movie. Before we knew it, Hollywood was a Hollywood movie star.

www.summerbridgeactivities.com   **Reading Connection—Grade 3—RBP3829**

Read and Think

1. What did Hollywood do that was unusual?
   A. He could run very fast.
   B. He could jump very high.
   C. He could jump on a moving truck.

2. How did the Hollywood dog trainer find out about Hollywood the dog?
   A. He saw him jump in the mail truck.
   B. He read about him in the newspaper.
   C. He used to be a mail carrier.

Word Attack

1. What does the word <u>peculiar</u> mean?
   A. bad
   B. strange
   C. good

Try to Apply

1. Why is Hollywood a good name for this dog?

   _____

   _____

2. Describe a trick that your pet or a pet that you know can do.

   _____

   _____

   _____

   _____

Language Skills

Words that tell about something are called **adjectives**. Write the correct adjective in the blank.

1. _____ dogs bark at cars.
   one   some

2. Hollywood has a _____ habit.
   second   strange

3. The newspaper put his picture on the _____ page.
   first   back

4. An _____ trainer needed Hollywood for a movie.
   angry   animal

5. Before his _____ birthday Hollywood was famous.
   mom's   second

Rewrite each group of words using 's or (') to show who owns something.
Ex.   movie by Art
<u>Art's movie</u>

6. peculiar habit of Hollywood

   _____

7. article by the reporter

   _____

8. tricks of the animals

   _____

9. a movie with Hollywood

   _____

Where Are We Going?

1   Where are we going? Do you know if it's far?
     Let's go to a place where there is no more war.

2   To a land past the sea and far away.
     To a land where freedom can't be taken away.

3   To a land where the mountains tower so high.
     To a land where blue is the color of the sky.

4   To a land where the deserts are sunny and dry.
     To a land where golden eagles fly.

5   To a land where the clouds are fluffy and white.
     To a land where beaches are a beautiful sight.

6   To a land where the fields of corn grow tall.
     To a land where freedom is a gift to all.

www.summerbridgeactivities.com   **Reading Connection—Grade 3—RBP3829**

Read and Think

1. Do you think a place like the one described in this poem is real? Explain your answer.

   _____

   _____

   _____

2. Whom do you think is writing this poem?
   A. someone who likes to travel
   B. someone from the United States
   C. someone from a country that doesn't have the freedoms that America has

3. Write about how you think a perfect place would be.

   _____

   _____

Word Attack

1. What does the word <u>tower</u> mean in this poem?
   A. a tall building
   B. to stand tall

Find words from the poem that have the long <u>i</u> sound. Write each word in the correct group.

2. long <u>i</u> spelled with <u>y</u>

   _____

   _____

   _____

3. long <u>i</u> spelled <u>i</u> consonant <u>e</u>

   _____

4. long <u>i</u> spelled with <u>igh</u>

   _____

   _____

Language Skills

Some words can be a noun or a verb. Circle **Y** if the underlined word is used the same way it is in the poem. Circle **N** if it is not. The paragraph is in ( ).

1. <u>Place</u> (1) that bag on the counter.
   Y   N

2. We went <u>past</u> (2) that house yesterday.
   Y   N

3. That is the world's tallest <u>tower</u> (3).
   Y   N

4. A <u>fly</u> (4) buzzed around her head.
   Y   N

5. Our plane is going to <u>land</u> (6) on time.
   Y   N

Adjectives describe nouns. They tell size, color, and shape. Rewrite each sentence using one of the adjectives in place of the underlined words. Hint: The new adjectives are synonyms of the underlined words.

bright	pale	tall
arid	puffy	gorgeous

6. To a land where the mountains tower so <u>high</u>.

   _____

   _____

7. To a land where the deserts are <u>sunny</u> and <u>dry</u>.

   _____

   _____

Ellis Island

1   Located in New York Harbor, Ellis Island was once used as the entrance to America. It was nicknamed the "Golden Door." Between 1897 and 1938, about 15 million people came from other countries to America. They came in search of religious freedom. They came hoping for a prosperous new life. They came to find the "American Dream."

2   When people from other countries came to Ellis Island, they arrived by boat. These people were called immigrants. When the boats arrived at the island, immigration officers greeted the immigrants. Immigrants had to have health records and papers from their home countries in order to pass through immi-gration. There were doctors giving physicals to verify the health records. Many immigrants passed the inspection and entered the United States. Other immigrants were sent away.

3   Many immigrants who entered the country were often disappointed. They didn't earn a lot of money and often had trouble finding places to live. They found that many Americans did not welcome them. They felt that they were not given the same rights as other Americans. It took many years for the immigrants to receive rights and privileges in the United States. Still, many immigrants felt the wait was worth it. Ellis Island is now a historical landmark.

    www.summerbridgeactivities.com

Read and Think

1. What is Ellis Island?

   A. a door with golden arches

   B. the entrance to America for immigrants

   C. an island where immigrants live

2. Why did people come to America from other countries?

   _____

3. Put a **T** if the sentence is true. Put an **F** if the sentence is false.

   _____ Between 1897 and 1938 people traveled to Ellis Island by ship, air-plane, and train.

   _____ People came to America in search of religious freedom and a prosperous new life.

   _____ Immigrants had to have health records and papers from their home countries.

   _____ If immigrants had health papers, they were accepted into America.

   _____ Everyone who came to America was allowed to come in.

4. What is an <u>immigrant</u>?

   A. an American citizen

   B. someone who came from another country to America

   C. someone who worked at Ellis Island

5. From what you have read "American Dream" probably means

   A. a new television show.

   B. a better way of life.

   C. what Americans dream while they sleep.

Try to Apply

1. What country or countries are your ancestors from?

   _____

   _____

   _____

Word Attack

Draw a line between the syllables of each word.

1. prosperous
2. countries
3. immigration
4. inspection
5. disappointed
6. Americans
7. entrance
8. officers

An **antonym** is a word that means the opposite of another word. Find the word in the paragraph in ( ) that means the opposite of each word. Write the word in the blank.

9. lose (1) _____

10. failed (2) _____

11. taking (2) _____

12. exit (3) _____

The Statue of Liberty is a main attraction of Liberty Island. The statue is a symbol of freedom and liberty. In its early days, it welcomed immigrants from all over the world. "From her beacon-hand Glows world-wide welcome" is just part of the poem written on the base of the enormous statue.

The Statue of Liberty was a gift from the French people. It was presented to the United States on July 4, 1884. The statue was given to celebrate the United States' independence from Britain. The French fought with the Americans during the War of Independence. The French armies helped the United States win the war.

The Statue of Liberty stands 152 feet from the base to her torch. Her waist is 35 feet around. Her index finger alone is eight feet long. Her smile is three feet wide. The total weight of the statue is about 225 tons.

The statue was built in France. It was then taken apart and shipped to the United States. It took 214 large crates to transport the enormous statue.

Read and Think

1. What is the Statue of Liberty a symbol of?

   A. the friendship between France and the United States

   B. freedom and liberty

   C. the friendliness of the American people

2. Put a **T** if the sentence is true. Put an **F** if the sentence is false.

   _____ The Statue of Liberty was a welcome sight to many immigrants.

   _____ The statue was given to celebrate the United States' independence from France.

   _____ The French fought alongside the Americans in the War of Independence.

   _____ The Statue of Liberty's smile is three feet wide.

   _____ The statue was built in the United States, then shipped to France.

3. What does independence mean in this reading?

   A. freedom

   B. celebration

4. In paragraph one, "In its early days" probably means

   A. when the statue was a baby.

   B. when the statue was first reassembled in America.

   C. in the morning hours.

5. The Statue of Liberty was transported in crates because

   A. it was a surprise present.

   B. everyone loves a puzzle.

   C. it was too large to ship in one piece.

Word Attack

1. Put a √ by synonyms of the word big.

   _____ enormous

   _____ huge

   _____ gigantic

   _____ tiny

   _____ large

   _____ petite

   _____ colossal

   _____ miniature

   _____ immense

2. The meaning of a word may change depending on how the word is used in a sentence. Read each sentence. Write the letter for the correct definition of each underlined word on the line.

   A. a gift   **B.** to give   **C.** to send

   _____ The French gave the United States a present.

   _____ The French will present the Statue of Liberty to the United States.

Language Skills

Write each sentence in the correct order. Remember to begin each sentence with a capital letter and end with the correct punctuation mark.

1. weighed I 225 believe tons can't statue the

   _____

   _____

2. stands Liberty for the all for freedom of Statue

   _____

   _____

Chinese Immigrants

China is a very large country. Many people live in China. In the late 1800s, overcrowded towns and villages in China meant there wasn't much food. The Chinese people were paying most of the money they earned to the government. They couldn't earn enough money to care for their families. During this time, many Chinese men moved to America with dreams of wealth and prosperity.

The Chinese men discovered that America wasn't the "Golden Door" they expected. Many Americans in the west were digging for gold. Many were striking it rich. The immigrants from China wanted to strike it rich, too. But the Chinese men weren't allowed to claim the gold. Some Americans would hire the Chinese men to dig for gold. They paid the Chinese men a very small salary, but they wouldn't let

the Chinese immigrants have any rights to the gold. Many Chinese decided to start their own businesses. One profitable business was the laundry service.

The women remained in China to take care of the children and the family-owned land. As the children grew older, the boys were sent to the United States to work with their fathers and grandfathers.

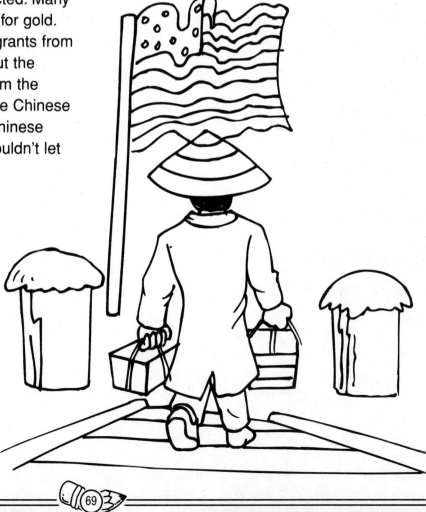

Read and Think

1. What is the main idea?
   A. Many people were getting rich by digging for gold.
   B. China is a large country.
   C. Chinese immigrants in the 1800s found life in America difficult.

2. Why were the Chinese men coming to America in the 1800s?

   _____

   _____

3. Why didn't the Chinese women come with the Chinese men to America?

   _____

   _____

4. What does the word <u>prosperity</u> mean?
   A. success
   B. land
   C. laundry service

Word Attack

Write the two words that each contraction stands for.

1. didn't   _____ _____

2. wasn't   _____ _____

3. weren't   _____ _____

4. couldn't   _____ _____

Read each sentence. Add *-ing* to the word in ( ). Then write the word in the blank.

5. Working people in China couldn't make a decent _____. (live)

6. Chinese immigrants tried _____ for gold. (dig)

7. Many people were _____ it rich. (strike)

8. Americans were _____ the Chinese little money to work. (pay)

9. One way of _____ money was to open a laundry. (earn)

Language Skills

Underline the **helping verb**. Then circle the **S** if the subject is singular or **P** if the subject is plural.

1. Many people are living in China.
   S   P

2. A Chinese citizen was paying a lot of money to the Chinese government.
   S   P

3. Many Americans were digging for gold.
   S   P

4. When a boy grew old enough he was sent to America.
   S   P

5. His mother is waiting in China.
   S   P

Ling-Shau Yu's Journal

June 15, 1926

I am so excited. I am going to go with my grandfather to the New World. I had to beg my mother to allow me to go. I want to see my father. He has been in the New World for two years. I wonder what the New World is like. I wonder why my father left us to go to the New World.

June 20, 1926

This morning I said good-bye to my mother and grandmother. I said good-bye to my homeland, China. I will miss my mother and grandmother. I will miss China. My mother cried, and my grandmother went back inside the house. My grandfather and I got on a huge boat. It was the biggest boat I have ever seen. Many other people got on the boat, too. They are all going to the New World. Grandfather says that the trip will be long. Grandfather says I should be patient. I am not patient. I want to be in the New World now. I want to see my father. I want to help my father with his new laundry business.

August 5, 1926

We have finally reached America. The boat trip was harder than I expected. I became very sick, and I had to lie down most of the time. I miss my grandmother and mother. There are many people here. Everyone looks very different from people in my country. A doctor looked down my throat. Other people checked my paperwork and made my grandfather sign many papers. My grandfather told me to be polite. I tried to be polite, but it was hard. I want to see my father.

August 8, 1926

Today I found my father. He was glad to see us. We hugged and we cried. It was good to be in his arms again. He took us to his home. It had two bedrooms. Grandfather got his own bedroom, and Father and I share a room. I don't have anymore time to write. Father is taking us to his shop to work. It is good to be in the New World. It is good to be with my father. I hope that my mother and grandmother will be coming to America soon.

© RBP Books   www.summerbridgeactivities.com   Reading Connection—Grade 3—RBP3829

Read and Think

1. Why is Ling-Shau Yu writing a journal?
   - A. to tell about his trip to America
   - B. his mother wanted him to
   - C. to practice his writing

2. What is the New World?
   - A. an undiscovered land
   - B. America
   - C. China

3. Complete each sentence.
   - A. Ling-Shau's homeland is

     _____.
   - B. Ling-Shau's father started a

     _____ business.
   - C. Ling-Shau traveled by

     _____ to the New World.
   - D. Ling-Shau traveled with his

     _____ to the New World.

4. About how long did Ling-Shau's trip to the New World take?
   - A. seven weeks
   - B. seven months
   - C. seven years

Word Attack

Write the two words that make up each compound word.

1. grandfather   _____   _____
2. paperwork   _____   _____
3. bedroom   _____   _____
4. grandmother   _____   _____

Language Skills

Words like *after, although, because, until,* and *while* can be used to combine two sentences. Choose one word to help combine the two sentences into one. Then write the new sentence.

after	although	until
while	because	

1. I am so excited. I am going to go with my grandfather to the New World.

   _____

   _____

2. A doctor looked down my throat. Other people checked my paperwork.

   _____

   _____

3. I am not patient. Grandfather says the trip will be long.

   _____

   _____

4. My mother cried. My grandfather and I got on a huge boat.

   _____

   _____

5. He took us home. We hugged and cried.

   _____

   _____

Try to Apply

Imagine you are traveling to live in a new country. Write a page in your journal telling what you think it will be like. Remember to put the date at the top of the page.

My Summer Vacation

Summer Vacation Report by Ming Ho

1   Have you ever tried to build a wall with blocks? The Chinese built a huge one. My family and I traveled to China for summer vacation. My favorite part was when we walked on the Great Wall of China. Grandmother says it is one of the seven man-made wonders of the world. Can you believe it is more than 2,000 years old and 4,500 miles long?

2   Part of the Great Wall of China is near the capital city of Beijing. My father grew up there. One of China's emperors decided to build a wall around China to keep out enemies. The teachers did not like the emperor because he burned books. So he made artists, writers, and teachers work hard to help build the wall. A lot of people worked on the wall their whole life.

3   Our guide said it took 1,000 years to build the wall. It is really made of many walls built at different times and connected together. Every part of it was made by hand. People used stone, bricks, and dirt. About one billion people helped to build China's Great Wall. To find out how wide the wall is, try this. Stand ten men next to each other. That is how wide it is. The wall is as tall as five men. Many people died helping build the wall. Its nickname is the "Long Graveyard." Can you guess why?

4   My cousin Cho and I loved the watchtowers. They are two stories high. The Chinese soldiers could see their enemies from there. People and nature have ruined a lot of the wall, which is sad. But tourists still travel to see it. Astronauts can even see the wall from orbit. Someday, maybe I will, too.

www.summerbridgeactivities.com   Reading Connection—Grade 3—RBP3829

Read and Think

Circle **T** if the sentence is true. Circle **F** if the sentence is false.

1. The Great Wall of China is 2,500 miles long.
   T   F

2. Part of the wall is near China's capital, Beijing.
   T   F

3. The teachers did not like the emperor because he was not Chinese.
   T   F

4. It took 1,000 years to build the wall.
   T   F

5. Ming and Cho loved the towers on the wall.
   T   F

Word Attack

Find the word in the paragraph number in ( ) that fits the definition.

1. liked best _____(1)

2. entire _____(2)

3. to place in an upright position _____(3)

4. to circle around _____(4)

Draw a line between the syllables of each word.

5. v a c a t i o n

6. g r a n d m o t h e r

7. e m p e r o r

8. c o n n e c t e d

9. a s t r o n a u t s

Language Skills

Some words, like *I, she, he, we, it,* and *they,* are used in place of other words. They are called **pronouns**.

Example

My family and I went to China for summer vacation.

The word <u>I</u> is used in place of <u>Ming</u>.

Read each sentence. Fill in the blank.

1. My family went to China. We walked on the Great Wall.
   <u>We</u> stands for _____.

2. The emperor burned books. He made teachers help build the wall.
   <u>He</u> stands for _____.

3. The wall is 2,000 years old. It is different walls connected together.
   <u>It</u> stands for _____.

4. Cho and I loved the watchtowers. They are two stories high.
   <u>They</u> stands for _____.

Pen Pal Letter

May 7, 2002

Dear Ming,

Life here in Queensland, Australia, has been a lot of the same old thing. That is, until yesterday. Yesterday, my class went on a field trip to the Great Barrier Reef. The reef is a different kind of school. It was a great place to study. Our trip reminded me about your trip to the Great Wall of China.

We took a boat out, and then we took turns scuba diving. It was so much fun. I have never seen so many beautiful plants and animals before. I learned a lot about life in the ocean.

Did you know the Great Barrier Reef is one of the seven natural wonders of the world? It is 1,200 miles long and 45 miles wide in places. Astronauts have taken pictures of it from outer space. But the reef is really 2,500

reefs hooked together. The boat captain said it is nearly one million years old. Wow!

I couldn't believe how beautiful it was underwater. The colors were amazing, and I have never seen so much coral in my life. The reef is made of the hard skeletons of tiny animals called polyps.

There were so many kinds of coral that I had to stop counting at 50. There are mushroom coral, leather coral, table coral, and one of my favorites, the brain coral. Carlson Devon asked Jimmy Fitz if he wanted to take a brain home with him to help him do his homework. Ha! Ha! Hey, Ming, my mom says it's bedtime. I'll finish this tomorrow. G'night, mate.

www.summerbridgeactivities.com   **Reading Connection—Grade 3—RBP3829**

Read and Think

1. Number the sentences in the order they happened.

   _____ Mom says it is bedtime.

   _____ The class went on a field trip.

   _____ They took turns scuba diving.

   _____ Carlson asks Jimmy if he wants to take home a brain.

Circle the correct answer.

2. This part of the letter is mainly about
   _____.

   A. the Great Wall of China

   B. the seven natural wonders of the world

   C. the Great Barrier Reef

Circle **T** if the sentence is true. Circle **F** if the sentence is false.

3. Life in Queensland has been pretty boring until yesterday.
   T   F

4. The Great Barrier Reef is incredible.
   T   F

5. Coral is pretty dull to look at.
   T   F

6. There were skeletons all over under the water.
   T   F

7. Carlson Devon had a headache and couldn't do his homework.
   T   F

Word Attack

1. Number the words in the order they would be found in the dictionary.

   _____ astronauts

   _____ counting

   _____ polyps

   _____ Australia

   _____ coral

   _____ reef

Language Skills

Write **N** if the word is a noun. Write **V** if the word is a verb.

   _____ **1.** took

   _____ **2.** learned

   _____ **3.** boat

   _____ **4.** reef

   _____ **5.** counting

   _____ **6.** astronaut

   _____ **7.** coral

   _____ **8.** believe

Pen Pal Letter, continued

1   Okay, I'm back. Now, where was I? Oh, yeah. Really, living on the reef is not a laughing matter. It is really dangerous for the animals there. Mrs. Garvey said many of the fish take a partner. That is like when we do seat work together in class.

2   A remora is a fish that cleans sharks by sucking the shark's skin. The remora gets a free ride. The shark also protects it from other fish that might try to eat it.

3   Then there is the clown fish. It lives between the stinging tentacles of the anemone. Even though the anemone usually kills small fish, it leaves the clown fish alone. No one knows why.

4   My favorite partner is the fish that swims into the mouths of bigger fish. It eats food from between the bigger fish's teeth. The dentist gets a meal, and the other fish gets its teeth cleaned for free!

5   Another way fish are protected is by swimming in schools. Larger fish, like the barracuda, will go after a fish swimming alone. Mrs. Garvey said, "In the reef, just like at home, it is wise not to go places alone."

6   Remember I said the reef was so colorful? We found out some fish use their color so well, they blend right in. They also use color to hide so they can catch a meal. It's kind of like camouflage.

7   Ming, you would not believe the amazing animals on the reef. There are fish that weigh 1,000 pounds. They are called marlins. There are giant clams that weigh 500 pounds and are four feet around. Our guide said a kid accidentally walked into one, and the clam closed up. Mrs. Garvey laughed and said it was just a joke.

8   We saw a parrot fish. Its mouth has a sharp edge like a parrot's beak. It can bite off the hard coral and eat the polyps inside.

9   The most amazing thing I saw was a loggerhead turtle. It swam right by us. It was six feet long. Did you know that only one in 5,000 baby sea turtles lives? I guess the turtles must taste good.

10   Well, I have to go eat dinner. We're having turtle soup. Just kidding! Write soon.

Your pen pal,
Stella Grant

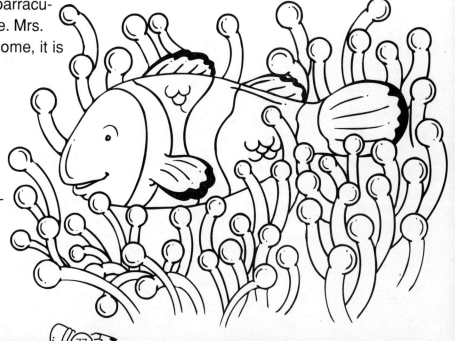

Read and Think

1. List three ways fish on the Great Barrier Reef can protect themselves.

   A. _____

   B. _____

   C. _____

You can often figure out the meaning of a word by looking at the words around it. Read the paragraph numbered in ( ). Circle the correct answer.

2. The word <u>camouflage</u> (6) probably means
   A. a game of hide and seek.
   B. using your camera underwater.
   C. blending into the world around you.

3. The main idea of Stella's letter is
   A. scuba diving is fun.
   B. the ocean is a dangerous place.
   C. the Great Barrier Reef is a beautiful place with many different types of animals.

Word Attack

The ending -**er** often means "more." Sometimes it is used to compare two things. The ending -**est** means "most." It is used to compare more than two things. Write -*er* or -*est* in the blank.

1. The clown fish is small _____ than the shark.

2. We saw the great _____ clam of all at the reef.

Underline the three words in each row that belong.

3. clam   marlin   seagull   anemone

4. swim   walk   ride   school

Write the base word for each word below. When the ending -**ed** or -**ing** is added to some words, a silent *e* is dropped, or a final consonant is doubled.

5. living _____   9. cleaned _____

6. laughing _____   10. swimming _____

7. striking _____   11. amazing _____

8. stinging _____   12. kidding _____

Study Hall

The **index** of a book is usually at the back. It lists the book's topics in alphabetical order. It also lists the number of the page each topic can be found on. Use the index to help answer the questions below.

   anemone, 5, 42
   coral, 2, 28–30
   partnerships, 42, 57–60
   turtles, 37–38

1. On what page would you find two of the listed topics? _____

2. On what pages could you find out about baby loggerhead turtles? _____

3. What could you learn about on pages 28–30? _____

September 19, 2002

Dear Stella,

Thanks for your letter. It sounds like we have both been having a great time. Did Jimmy Fitz ever get the brain he needed? Ha, ha! Oh yeah, now I remember. You aren't supposed to remove things from the reef.

I watched a show on TV that said the Great Barrier Reef is endangered. I guess people visiting there can hurt the reef by boating, diving, and fishing. Did you know that the Great Wall of China is also in danger from natural things like the weather? In many spots it is crumbling, and you can hardly tell it's a wall.

My grade at school is doing a geography fair in October. It is at night, and everyone can come. We get to choose our own subject. Then we have to give a presentation. I decided to do mine on the Great Wall of China. My teacher also had a great idea. I am going to compare the Great Wall with the Great Barrier Reef. Isn't that cool! Thanks for all the info on the reef.

Each person in our class has to make a poster. Mrs. Grady is big into charts, so everyone's poster has to have one. I am sending you mine. But you have to finish it.

Good luck!

Your pal, Ming

Read and Think

Read the chart below. Make an **X** in the column under Great Wall of China if the characteristic tells something about the wall. Mark an **X** in the column under Great Barrier Reef if the characteristic tells about the reef. Fill out the chart that Ming sent Stella. Use what you have read before to help.

Let's Settle Our Differences

Characteristics	Great Wall of China	Great Barrier Reef
1. Man-made wonder		
2. 4,500 miles long		
3. 45 miles wide		
4. Billions of polyps died to make this		
5. Found on land		
6. Built in sections		
7. Natural wonder		
8. Seen from space		
9. 1,200 miles long		
10. Many men died building this		
11. Visited by tourists		
12. 1,000,000 years old		
13. 1,000 years to build		
14. Found in the ocean		
15. Ten-men wide		
16. Endangered		

A **Venn diagram** is used to make an organized picture of what you have read. It uses two circles that overlap to compare two things. Each circle contains facts about each thing. The part that overlaps has facts that are the same for both things.

17. Fill out the Venn diagram below. Use the facts from the filled out chart.

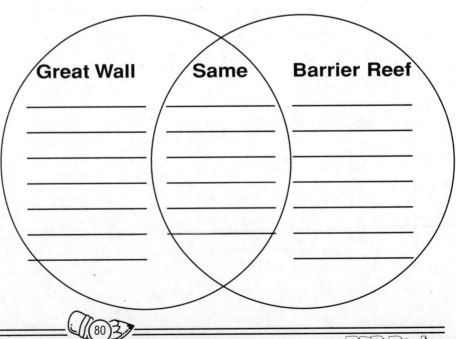

Florida is located in the southeastern part of the United States. It is a <u>peninsula</u>. A peninsula is like an island because it is almost completely surrounded by water. But unlike an island, Florida is bordered by land on the northern part. Georgia and Alabama share borders with Florida. When Spanish explorers settled there, they called the area Florida because of all the flowers. <u>Florida</u> is a Spanish word for flowers.

This part of the United States is known for its warm climate and wonderful beaches.

Florida's nickname is the Sunshine State. Because of the nice weather, it is a popular place to visit. Florida has grown over the years. Today it is the home of several amusement parks.

Florida produces lots of food. It is best known for its fruit and fruit juices. Over half of the United States' orange and grapefruit juice is processed in Florida. The warm climate allows the fruit to grow all year.

Read and Think

1. Where is Florida?
   A. in Spain
   B. in Georgia
   C. in the southeastern part of the United States

2. _____ and _____ share a border with Florida.

3. Complete each sentence.
   A. Florida is a Spanish word for _____.

   B. Florida is located in the _____ part of the United States.

   C. _____ explorers settled in Florida.

   D. Florida produces a lot of _____ and _____.

4. What is a peninsula?
   A. the Spanish word for pencil
   B. land that is almost completely surrounded by water
   C. the same thing as an island

Word Attack

1. Combine the words in the columns below to make compound words.

   south   fruit

   grape   shine

   sun   east

   _____

   _____

   _____

Language Skills

Some words can be used as either a noun or a verb. Write **N** if the underlined word is used as a noun. Write **V** if the word is a verb.

1. A peninsula is surrounded on three sides by water. _____
   Mom said to water all the plants. _____

2. Sandra can part her hair in the middle. _____

   Florida is bordered by land on the northern part. _____

3. Georgia and Alabama share borders with Florida. _____
   Amy got her share of the candy. _____

4. Florida does produce lots of food. _____
   Can you tell me if tomatoes are in the produce section? _____

5. Florida is a Spanish word for flowers. _____
   That plant flowers around Christmastime. _____

The County Fair

1 I love to go to the county fair,
I love the noises and the smells in the air.

2 The people, the animals, and the food,
All create a festive mood.

3 You can hear the animals in the shed,
Calling out loudly to be fed.

4 The barkers holler, "Come on and play,
I bet you're feeling lucky today."

5 The Ferris wheel spins high in the sky.
It makes me feel like I can fly.

6 The rides are fast and so exciting,
Especially the one they call Blue Lightning.

7 Hot dogs, drinks, and cotton candy,
The vendors sell and make so handy.

8 I love to go to the county fair,
I love the fun and excitement there.

©RBP Books   www.summerbridgeactivities.com   Reading Connection—Grade 3—RBP3829

Read and Think

1. How does the author feel about the county fair?
   A. The author enjoys the county fair.
   B. The author thinks the county fair is boring.
   C. The author thinks the county fair is overwhelming.

2. How do you feel about a county fair?

   _____

   _____

3. Use your senses and the poem to think about a county fair.

   A. Write two things you can <u>see</u>.

   _____   _____

   B. Write two things you can <u>hear</u>.

   _____   _____

   C. Write two things you can <u>smell</u>.

   _____   _____

   D. Write two things you can <u>touch</u>.

   _____   _____

   E. Write two things you can <u>taste</u>.

   _____   _____

4. What does the word <u>vendor</u> mean?
   A. a person who sells
   B. a person who runs the rides
   C. a person who manages the county fair

Word Attack

Write a word from the poem that rhymes with each word below. Then think of another word that rhymes.

1. fair   _____   _____

2. shed   _____   _____

3. sky   _____   _____

4. play   _____   _____

Write the word in verse number ( ) that is the antonym of the meaning below.

5. quiet (1) _____

6. unfortunate (4) _____

7. not quick (6) _____

8. to dislike strongly (8) _____

Language Skills

Some verbs do not form the past tense by adding -ed. They change their form. These are called **irregular verbs**. Write the correct form of the verb in ( ) in the blank.

1. They had _____ the animals in the shed. (hear)

2. I wondered if they _____ lucky. (feel)

3. The Ferris wheel _____ high in the sky after Chuck and Ryan climbed in. (spin)

4. The vendors _____ a lot of hot dogs and cotton candy at last week's fair. (sell)

5. I _____ to the county fair yesterday. (go)

Sue and her mother always bake a cherry pie for the county fair. They enter their pie in the pie contest, and, more often than not, Sue and her mother win. The fair is one month away. Sue and her mother are beginning to make plans for the best cherry pie ever.

Each year Sue and her mother try many variations of their prize pie. They have tried using canned cherries. They have tried using fresh cherries from their cherry tree. They have tried using cherries that had been frozen for several months. The cherries fresh from the tree always taste best. Sue and her mother have tried using different amounts of

sugar in the cherry filling. They always settle on the amount that makes the pie sweet and tart. They have also tried different types of crust. The first type of crust was thick and doughy. It made a big, puffy baked crust on top with cherry juice oozing out from the top of the pie. The second crust was flakier. The top of the pie was made of strips of dough woven over and under. They decided on the flakier crust.

On the day of the county fair, Sue and her mother bake their cherry pie. They enter it in the pie contest, and once again their pie wins first place. They succeed in making the best cherry pie ever.

Read and Think

1. What is the main idea?
   A. choosing cherries for a cherry pie
   B. making the best cherry pie ever
   C. going to the county fair

2. Which type of pie did Sue and her mother bake for the county fair this year?
   A. a sweet pie with a flaky crust and fresh cherries
   B. a sweet and tart pie with a flaky crust and canned cherries
   C. a sweet and tart pie with a flaky crust and fresh cherries

3. How long before the fair do Sue and her mother begin working on their pie?

   _____

   _____

   _____

4. What does <u>succeed</u> mean?
   A. to do what you set out to do
   B. to eat a watermelon, seeds and all
   C. to fail at what you try to do

Circle **F** for fact or **O** for opinion.

5. Sue and her mother always bake a cherry pie for the fair.
   F   O

6. The second crust was flakier.
   F   O

7. They succeed in making the best cherry pie ever.
   F   O

Language Skills

Words that tell about something are called **adjectives**. Write three adjectives that tell about the words below.

1. cherries   _____ | _____
2. pie crust _____ | _____
3. pie   _____ | _____

Word Attack

Add the correct suffix to each word.

1. cherry + s   _____
2. pie + s   _____
3. crust + s   _____
4. flaky + er   _____
5. doughy + er _____
6. decide + ed _____

The ending **-er** often means "more." Sometimes it is used to compare two things. The ending **-est** means "most." It is used to compare more than two things. Write the correct form of the word in each column. Two of the words are tricky.

	-er	-est
7. good		
8. flaky		
9. sweet		
10. thick		
11. puffy		

Reading Connection—Grade 3—RBP3829   www.summerbridgeactivities.com   ©RBP Books

The Runt

Every spring my dad lets me choose one of the piglets from the litter to raise. I raise the piglet to show at the county fair. Pigs that show well at the fair sell for a good price. Dad lets me keep the money I earn from the pig, so I work hard each year to raise my pig.

This year our sow had nine piglets. I usually choose the biggest and the strongest of the litter, but this year the runt caught my eye. The runt is the littlest pig of the litter. Usually the runt is too small to make its way to the sow to feed, so the runt dies because it doesn't get enough milk.

But this runt was a fighter. I sat in the pen watching the piglets step over each other. They were fighting to be first to the sow. The runt, however, came and nuzzled up to me. It was as if he thought that I had milk for him. I picked the runt up and took him to the house. Dad was surprised that I picked the runt of the litter. But I told Dad that I would make this runt into a prize pig.

Through the spring and summer I hand-fed the runt. He grew and grew. By fall he was ready to eat slop and grain. I took good care of my little pig. By spring, the little runt had grown into the biggest pig I had ever seen. My little runt won a first prize at the county fair. He wasn't so little anymore.

www.summerbridgeactivities.com Reading Connection—Grade 3—RBP3829

Read and Think

1. What is the main idea of the story?
   A. raising a runt
   B. growing up on a farm
   C. going to the fair

2. Put a **T** if the sentence is true. Put an **F** if the sentence is false.

   _____ The runt always grows up to be the biggest pig of the litter.

   _____ The runt won first prize at the fair.

   _____ The writer of the story earns money from selling pigs.

   _____ The sow had nine piglets.

3. Draw a line between the word and its definition.

   piglet   a group of baby pigs from one mother

   sow   to help grow up

   litter   cuddled

   nuzzled   baby pig

   raised   mother pig

4. What is a <u>runt</u> in this story?
   A. a type of candy
   B. the smallest piglet in a litter
   C. the biggest piglet in a litter

5. What does the idiom "caught my eye" mean?
   A. got something in my eye
   B. scared me
   C. got my attention

Study Hall

Some words have more than one meaning. The different meanings are numbered in the dictionary. Read each word and its meanings. Write the number of the correct meaning after each sentence.

> **raise** 1. To care for a baby until it is an adult.
> 2. To lift something up.

1. Mrs. Crosby said to <u>raise</u> your hand. _____

2. I am going to <u>raise</u> my puppy, Sinbad. _____

> **pen** 1. An instrument used to write with.
> 2. A fenced-in area where an animal is kept.

3. Marley took my green <u>pen</u> to do her homework. _____

4. There are six piglets in the <u>pen</u>. _____

> **slop** 1. Food given to animals. 2. What happens when a liquid spills over the sides of a container.

5. Teresa tried to be careful, but I saw the soup <u>slop</u> out of the bowl. _____

6. Lexi gathered up the scraps of food for the pigs' <u>slop</u>. _____

Try to Apply

Choose a pet you would like to raise. Make a list of five things you would have to do to care for your pet.

Reading Connection—Grade 3—RBP3829   www.summerbridgeactivities.com   ©RBP Books

The Roller Coaster

The roller coaster's like a snake,
coiling 'round and 'round.
As the cars make their way up,
my heart begins to pound.

The big drop comes so quickly
I can't scream or yell.
The whipping of the curves
swings me like a bell.

As the ride comes to an end,
I start to smile and laugh.
I shout, "Let's go again
along that whipping path."

www.summerbridgeactivities.com Reading Connection—Grade 3—RBP3829

Read and Think

1. What is the poem about?

   _____

   _____

2. What does the writer of the poem compare the roller coaster to?

   _____

3. Why can't the writer of the poem scream or yell?

   A. because of a sore throat

   B. because ride operators ask you not to

   C. because the drop comes so quickly

Word Attack

The **apostrophe** in some words takes the place of one or more letters. Write the letter or letters that are missing in these words.

1. roller coaster's   _____

2. 'round   _____

3. can't   _____

4. let's   _____

A **synonym** is a word that means the same as another word. An **antonym** is a word that has the opposite meaning of another word. Put an **S** in the blank if the underlined word in the sentence is a synonym for the word given by the blank. Put an **A** if the word is an antonym.

5. Roller coasters <u>coil</u> like a snake.
   twist _____

6. The cars of the roller coaster rush <u>down</u>.
   above _____

7. The <u>big</u> drop happens quickly.
   huge _____

8. The ride finally comes to an <u>end</u>.
   beginning _____

9. I <u>smile</u>, laugh, and shout.
   grin _____

10. It follows the same <u>path</u> over and over.
    route _____

Write the correct letters in the blank to finish the sentence.

wh	sh	th	gh

11. We were all _____ipped from side to side on the coaster.

12. At the end everyone had a good lau_____.

13. A roller coaster has to follow the same pa_____ every time.

14. I never knew riding in a car could make you _____out.

Try to Apply

1. Describe a time that you rode a roller coaster. If you have never been on a roller coaster, use your imagination to write about what it might be like.

   _____

   _____

   _____

   _____

Fairy Tales

Come, read with me a fairy tale;
Board my ship and let's set sail.

Let's go to once upon a time,
Where good is good and all words rhyme.

Come, follow me to places afar,
beyond the moon, beyond the star.

We'll travel to lands so far away,
Where elves and fairies hide and play.

We'll pretend to be pirates who wander the sea,
Seeking adventure, wild and free.

Let's go where things are not as they seem,
To places we can only dream.

Read and Think

1. What is this poem about?
   A. going to faraway places
   B. reading fairy tales
   C. dreaming about faraway places

2. The people in the poem are going to travel
   A. on a spaceship.
   B. while they sleep.
   C. in their imagination.

Try to Apply

1. Are fairy tales real or make-believe?

   _____

Word Attack

1. Some words have more than one meaning.
   Read each sentence. Write the letter of the
   correct definition for each underlined word.
   A. to get on a ship
   B. pieces of wood
   C. a light in the sky
   D. the main actor, most important
   E. a piece of cloth used to propel a boat
   F. to float on the water

   _____ We used boards to build the ship.

   _____ The man boards the ship with his
   bags.

   _____ The star twinkled in the sky.

   _____ He is the star of the show.

   _____ They set sail for a trip over the
   ocean.

   _____ They made a sail for their boat.

Find words in the reading that have a long
vowel sound. Put them in the correct group
below.

2. long e spelled ea

   _____

   _____

   _____

3. long e spelled e

   _____

   _____

4. long e spelled ee

   _____

   _____

5. long a spelled ay

   _____

   _____

6. long a spelled ai

   _____

   _____

7. long a spelled a consonant e

   _____

   _____

8. long i spelled i consonant e

   _____

   _____

The Snow Maiden

1   Many years ago there lived an old woman and an old man. As they grew older, they also grew sadder, for they had no children. One winter morning, the old man looked out the window at the falling snow. "Let's build a snow child," he suggested to his wife. "Yes," said the old woman, "a snow maiden just for us."

2   The old man and the old woman went outside and began to make a little girl out of snow. They made her legs, her arms, and her head. They used bits of sparkling blue ice for her eyes. When the old man and old woman had finished, they stood back to look at what they had created. They could hardly believe their eyes. They had created a beautiful snow maiden. The old woman kissed the snow maiden gently on the cheek. Suddenly, the snow maiden began to smile. She stretched out her arms. Then she stretched out her legs. She spun around and gave a little laugh. "I'm alive," she giggled with delight. Then she ran and gave the old man and the old woman a hug. Nothing could have made the couple happier. At last, they had the child they had longed for.

3   The days passed. Soon the winter storms turned to spring showers. The sun began to warm the earth. The signs of spring were everywhere. But as the days became warmer, the snow maiden became more and more unhappy. She would not go outside. "Come, little daughter.

Why do you look so sad? Go outside and play with the other children," said the old woman to the snow maiden. The snow maiden did as she was told.

4   But before the snow maiden could join the other children, she disappeared. There was only a white mist where the girl had stood. The mist formed into a thin cloud and rose higher and higher until it joined the clouds in the sky. The old man and the old woman wept bitterly at the loss of their dear little snow maiden. Once again they were sad and lonely.

5   After a while, the days became shorter and the nights longer. The air was crisp and cool once again. Winter was coming. One night, as the first snow began to fall, the couple sat by the window remembering their dear little snow maiden. Suddenly, they heard a happy laugh and a familiar voice singing,

Winter is here. I am back with the snow.
Do not fear, when in the spring I go.
For I will return with the snow each year,
For you my parents are oh, so dear.

6   The couple ran to the door. They hugged their little snow maiden. How happy they were to be together again! The snow maiden stayed with them through each winter. Then, when spring came, she would disappear until winter returned to the old couple's cottage again.

© RBP Books   www.summerbridgeactivities.com   Reading Connection—Grade 3—RBP3829

Read and Think

1. Why were the old man and the old woman sad at the beginning of the story?
   - A. because they were growing old
   - B. because they had no children
   - C. because the winter was too cold

2. What brought the snow maiden to life?
   - A. a fairy godmother
   - B. a snowflake
   - C. the old woman's kiss

Write the **base word** for each word below. On another sheet of paper, add -*est* to each word and write a sentence with each word that compares more than two things.

6. warmer _____

7. happier _____

8. shorter _____

9. older _____

10. higher _____

Word Attack

The ending **-er** often means "more." Sometimes it is used to compare two things. The ending **-est** means "most." It is used to compare more than two things. Find the correct word to complete the sentence in the paragraph in ( ). Write it in the blank.

1. The days are getting_____ now that summer is here. (3)

2. That clown looks_____ than the one with the frowny face. (2)

3. Jessee's hair is _____ than Claudia's. (5)

4. Ilene is three years _____ than Kevin. (1)

5. That statue is _____ on the shelf than I thought. (4)

Try to Apply

1. Why would the snow maiden disappear in the spring?

   _____

   _____

   _____

2. What are some signs of spring?

   _____

   _____

   _____

3. What are some signs of winter?

   _____

   _____

   _____

Sweet Porridge

There was a poor but good little girl who lived with her mother in a small little house. One morning the mother went to the cupboard to find something to eat, but the cupboard was bare. So the mother sent the little girl into the forest to find some wild blueberries to eat.

While looking for berries, the girl met a woman. The woman was old and bent. She wore rags. She looked as if she hadn't eaten in days. The little girl felt sorry for the old woman. She gave the old woman all of her berries. As the woman ate the berries, something began to happen. The bent old woman changed into a beautiful enchanted fairy. The little girl could not believe her eyes.

"You have shown great kindness," said the enchanted fairy. "For your kindness I will give you this magic pot. When the magic words are said, sweet porridge will appear in the pot. With this magic pot you will never be hungry again. Simply say,

"Cook, little pot, cook.
Give us something to eat.
Cook, little pot, cook.
Give us something sweet."

The little girl thanked the fairy and took the pot home to her mother. The mother and the little girl were never hungry again. Instead they ate sweet porridge whenever they chose.

www.summerbridgeactivities.com
Reading Connection—Grade 3—RBP3829

Read and Think

1. What happened to the old woman when she ate the berries?
   A. She felt much better.
   B. She changed into an enchanted fairy.
   C. She thanked the little girl and went home.

2. Number the sentences in the order they happened in the story.
   ____ The little girl met an old woman.
   ____ She gave the little girl the magic pot.
   ____ The mother sent the little girl to find something to eat.
   ____ The old woman changed into an enchanted fairy.
   ____ The little girl gave the old woman the berries.

3. What does <u>enchanted</u> mean?
   A. magical
   B. chanting or singing
   C. mean

Try to Apply

1. Is this story real or make-believe?

   _____

2. If you had a magic pot, what would you want it to make?

   _____

   _____

   _____

Word Attack

A **compound word** is two words put together to make one. Choose from the words below to make compound words. Write the words in the blanks.

berries	board	thing	when
blue	ever	cup	some
	to	in	

1. _____ 2. _____

3. _____ 4. _____

5. _____

A **homophone** is a word that sounds the same as another word but is spelled differently and means something different. Choose the correct word; then write it in the blank.

6. Archer began to _____ the pancakes onto the griddle.
   pour   poor

7. All the pictures had been removed, and the walls were _____.
   bear   bare

8. After the accident, everyone walked as if they were in a _____.
   days   daze

9. Phillip asked Charlie if he could _____ the cheese.
   grate   great

10. Morris finally _____ some of the lasagna.
    eight   ate

Reading Connection—Grade 3—RBP3829   www.summerbridgeactivities.com   ©RBP Books

1   If fairy tales were real,
How strange life would be!

2   We'd make three wishes
And talk to fishes.
How strange life would be!

3   We'd play checkers with Snow White,
Follow pebbles in the night.
How strange life would be!

4   We'd kiss frogs and slay dragons,
Ride in coaches and wagons.
How strange life would be!

5   If fairy tales were real,
We'd have porridge every meal.
How strange life would be!

6   The magic is nice,
but I'd think twice
about living my life in a tale—

7   Or I might just find
myself in a bind
and living my life in a whale!

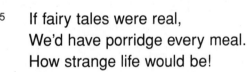

    www.summerbridgeactivities.com   **Reading Connection—Grade 3—RBP3829**

Read and Think

1. What is the main idea of this poem?

_____

_____

_____

Try to Apply

1. What do you think would be the strangest thing if fairy tales were real?

_____

_____

_____

Cross out the word that does not belong in each group.

2. Snow White   glass slipper
seven dwarfs   wicked queen

3. candy house   Hansel and Gretel
wicked witch   magic mirror

4. Prince Charming   glass slipper
poison apple   Cinderella

5. talking fish   Sleeping Beauty
spinning wheel   witches

6. Rapunzel   long hair
wicked stepsister   castle tower

7. If you had three wishes, what would they be?

_____

_____

_____

Word Attack

Find words in the poem that have a long <u>a</u> sound. Put the words in the correct group.

1. long <u>a</u> sound spelled <u>ay</u>

_____

2. long <u>a</u> sound spelled <u>a</u> consonant <u>e</u>

_____

_____

_____

Write the word in the verse in ( ) that is a synonym for each word listed below.

3. different (1)   _____

4. two (6)   _____

5. rocks (3)   _____

6. toads (4)   _____

7. cereal (5)   _____

8. lunch (5)   _____

9. tie (7)   _____

10. say (2)   _____

11. friendly (6)   _____

Finding Poochy

Jared's grandmother can be quite forgetful. She is always losing things. Sometimes she can't find her glasses when they are sitting on top of her head. Today she lost her little dog, Poochy. She ran some errands this morning, and she took Poochy with her. Now Poochy is missing. She asked Jared to help her find her dog. "Tell me everything you can remember, Grandma," said Jared. Jared took notes as his grandmother recalled her morning.

"I walked out my front door and turned east. My first stop was to return some books at a place with a flag flying outside the building.

"Then I went south and dropped off some cookies I had baked for Mrs. Green. She lives in a little house with a fence around the yard.

"Then I walked west to the grocery store and picked up a few items. Luckily I had a list so I remembered everything I needed. Poochy couldn't go into the store, so I tied him up outside by a tree.

"Then I walked north one block. I stopped at a shop with a large bench outside. I remember the bench because I was pretty tired by this time. I sat on the bench to take a rest. I finished my errand at the shop and came home. I haven't seen Poochy since I stopped at that shop. It's a shame, too, because I needed to take her in for a shampoo and cut."

"Grandma," said Jared, "I know where Poochy is."

www.summerbridgeactivities.com   Reading Connection—Grade 3—RBP3829

Read and Think

1. Where is Poochy?

   _____

   _____

   _____

2. What clues helped Jared find Poochy?

   _____

   _____

   _____

3. What does <u>recall</u> mean in this story?
   A. to do again
   B. to remember
   C. to find

4. Number the sentences in the order they happened.

   _____ I stopped at a shop with a large bench outside.

   _____ I dropped off some cookies at Mrs. Green's.

   _____ I returned some books to the library.

   _____ I tied Poochy outside by a tree.

   _____ I finished my errand at the shop.

Try to Apply

1. What building is west of Mrs. Green's house?

   _____

   _____

Word Attack

1. Draw a line between the opposites.

forget	small
east	right
north	found
left	remember
lost	south
large	west

Language Skills

Choose one word from each column to complete each sentence.

Subject	Verb	Object
I	tie	glasses
She	sat	dog
girl	lost	bench
Grandmother	find	outside

1. _____ can't _____ her _____ .

2. _____ has _____ her _____ , Poochy.

3. The _____ did _____ him _____ .

4. _____ _____ on the _____ .

Where in the World Is Ben?

1 My big brother Ben loves to travel the world. Every month he sends me a postcard. He never tells me where he is, though. He only gives me clues. Here is the latest postcard I received from Ben:

Dear Little Sister,

2 Guess where I am this month? Follow these clues to find me!

3 I had a great time last month in the country that is north of the United States. I flew across the Atlantic Ocean to a country where I saw the Eiffel Tower. From there I took a train south. I am in a country that looks like a boot on the map. I am enjoying eating lots of pasta.

4 Give my love to Mom and Dad. I'll be home soon.

Love,
Your brother Ben

The Best Little Sister in the World!
123 Elm Ave.
Salt Lake City, Utah
81234

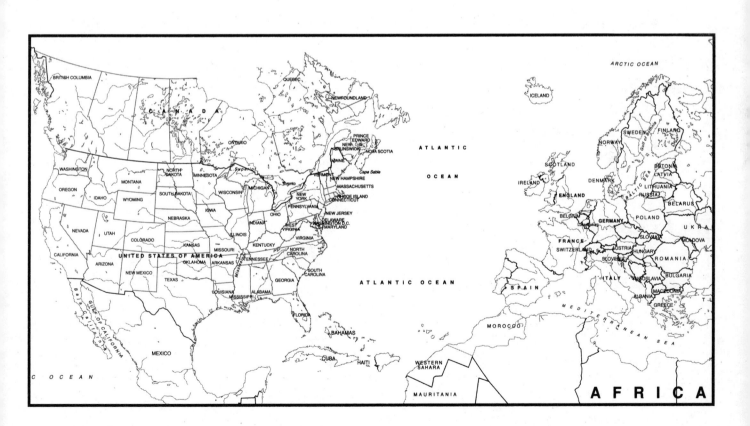

Read the clues on the postcard to help me find where my brother Ben is this month.

© RBP Books   www.summerbridgeactivities.com   Reading Connection—Grade 3—RBP3829

Read and Think

1. Where in the world is Ben?

   _____

   _____

2. What country is north of the United States?

   _____

   _____

3. Where did Ben fly when he crossed the Atlantic Ocean?

   _____

   _____

4. What continent is south of Italy?

   _____

   _____

Try to Apply

1. Write some clues to find a country on the map. Have a classmate follow your clues.

Language Skills

Put the correct punctuation at the end of each sentence.

   (.)   (?)   (!)

1. Can you find the country where Ben is hiding _____

2. Last month I traveled very far _____

3. Catch me if you can _____

4. The Eiffel Tower looks shorter from the plane _____

5. I can't believe we saw whales in the ocean _____

Some verbs do not form the past tense by adding -ed. They change their form. These are called **irregular verbs**. One form of the verb is listed after each sentence. Find the correct form of the verb in the paragraph in ( ). Write it in the blank.

6. Nelson _____ me a present from every place he visits.
   sent (1)

7. The pilot _____ the huge jet.
   fly (3)

8. She _____ really scary stories.   **told** (1)

9. _____ Jason his suitcase back, right now!   **gave** (4)

10. The policeman _____ a huge train wreck.   **see** (3)

Who's My Camp Counselor?

1   Going to camp is always the highlight of my summer. This year before I left for camp my counselor wrote me a letter. He told me in the letter how to recognize him, but when I got off the bus, it wasn't as easy as I thought it would be. Can you help me find my camp counselor?

Dear Camper,

I can't wait to see you next week at camp. You'll find me waiting for you when your bus arrives. I'll be wearing a camp counselor T-shirt, a baseball cap, shorts, and sneakers. I will be wearing sunglasses and a whistle around my neck. You can't miss me; I'm the handsome one.

Sincerely,
Your Counselor

Read and Think

1. Circle the correct camp counselor on page 103.

2. Put a **T** if the sentence is true. Put an **F** if the sentence is false.

   _____ The writer does not like to go to camp.

   _____ The camp counselor is wearing sandals.

   _____ The camp counselor is wearing sunglasses.

   _____ The camp counselor forgot his whistle.

   _____ The camper took a bus to camp.

3. What does <u>highlight</u> mean?
   A. a light that is high
   B. the best thing
   C. a summer activity

Try to Apply

List three things you would do if you were a counselor that would help the kids know which one you were.

1. _____

2. _____

3. _____

4. Why wasn't it easy for the camper to spot his counselor?

   _____

   _____

Word Attack

Write the two words that make up each contraction.

1. who's   _____ _____

2. wasn't   _____ _____

3. you'll   _____ _____

4. I'll   _____ _____

5. I'm   _____ _____

Language Skills

Some verbs do not form the past tense by adding -ed. They change their form. These are called **irregular verbs**. Find the correct form of the verb listed after each sentence. Look in the paragraph in ( ). Write the correct word in the blank.

1. I _____ my flashlight lying on my bed. **leave** (1)

2. You will _____ the right tent under the oak tree. **found** (1)

3. Jasmine _____ letters to her family when she was at camp. **write** (1)

4. You _____ we would have hot dogs cooked over a fire. **think** (1)

5. Our group _____ to go swimming for a reward last week. **get** (1)

Who's Prince Charming?

With the help of her fairy godmother, Cinderella makes it to the ball. But when she arrives, she is greeted by five handsome gentlemen. At first Cinderella becomes upset. She fears she will never find her prince. Then she remembers the handbook her fairy godmother gave her. She pulls it from her purse and begins reading it. Use the clues in the handbook to help Cinderella find the real Prince Charming.

How to Tell a Real Prince from a Fake
1. Real princes always wear a crown.
2. Real princes always wear a ring on their right hand.
3. Real princes never wear a wristwatch.
4. Real princes never wear sneakers.
5. Real princes always wear shirts with exactly seven buttons.

© RBP Books   www.summerbridgeactivities.com   Reading Connection—Grade 3—RBP3829

Read and Think

1. Circle the real Prince Charming on page 105.

2. How do you know the last handsome gentleman is not the handsome prince?

   _____

   _____

   _____

3. Put a **T** by the sentences that are true. Put an **F** by the sentences that are false.

   _____ The fairy godmother helped Cinderella get to the ball.

   _____ The fairy godmother gave Cinderella a handbook.

   _____ The real prince wears a wristwatch.

   _____ The real prince wears sneakers.

   _____ The real prince wears a crown and a ring on his right hand.

Word Attack

Write the two words that make up each compound word.

1. gentlemen   _____   _____

2. upset   _____   _____

3. handbook   _____   _____

4. godmother   _____   _____

5. wristwatch   _____   _____

Try to Apply

1. What else do you think might have been in the handbook the fairy godmother gave to Cinderella?

   _____

   _____

Language Skills

Underline the verb, circle the subject, and put an **X** on the object in each sentence.

1. Five gentlemen greet Cinderella.

2. The prince is wearing a crown.

3. She read the book of instructions.

4. The prince's shirt had seven buttons.

Word Attack

An **antonym** is a word that means the opposite of another word. Write the antonym of the underlined word in the blank.

1. The princes were all <u>handsome</u>.

   _____

2. At <u>first</u> Cinderella becomes upset.

   _____

3. She fears she will never <u>find</u> her prince.

   _____

4. Do you think Cinderella will <u>remember</u> her handbook? _____

What's for Dinner?

Mom's lunch meeting ran late. Not only is she exhausted, she isn't hungry. She decides to pick up fast food for the family. Everyone likes something different. She picks up a pizza, a taco, a hamburger, and some chicken. She leaves the food on the table and heads upstairs to soak in the tub. Read the clues to figure out who gets what to eat.

Dad will eat anything but pizza.
Brad will only eat chicken.
Chad and Tad will eat either pizza or a hamburger, but Chad prefers pizza.

Put an **X** in the box when you know someone does not eat a certain food. Put an **O** when you know someone does eat a certain food. As soon as you have an O in a square, put Xs across the row and down the column.

	pizza	taco	hamburger	chicken
Dad				
Brad				
Chad				
Tad				

www.summerbridgeactivities.com **Reading Connection—Grade 3—RBP3829**

Read and Think

1. What did each family member have for dinner?

   A. Dad _____

   B. Brad _____

   C. Chad _____

   D. Tad _____

2. Why didn't Mom feel like making dinner?
   A. She didn't know how to cook.
   B. Her family members are picky eaters.
   C. She was exhausted.

3. Who is the pickiest eater between Dad, Chad, Tad, and Brad? Explain your answer.

   _____

   _____

   _____

   _____

4. Number the sentences in the order they happened.

   _____ Mom heads upstairs to soak in the tub.

   _____ The food is left on the table.

   _____ She decides to pick up fast food.

   _____ The lunch meeting runs late.

   _____ Mom comes home.

Try to Apply

1. Which of those four foods is your favorite: pizza, chicken, taco, hamburger?

   _____

2. What fast food restaurant do you like to get food from?

   _____

Word Attack

1. What does prefer mean?
   A. like only
   B. would rather have
   C. do not like

Draw a line between the syllables of the foods listed below.

2. stro/ga/noff   6. burritos

3. lasagna   7. hamburger

4. casserole   8. guacamole

5. zucchini   9. omelet

Language Skills

Write five adjectives in the correct column describing each food.

chicken	pizza	taco	hamburger

The Pet Store Mix-Up

Martin is helping take care of his friend's pet store while his friend is on vacation. Martin has been doing a good job caring for the animals. Today he was cleaning out their cages. Unfortunately, Martin left the doors to four cages open, and the animals got out. Can you help Martin put the animals back into the right cages?

Neither the hamster nor the dog is in cage 4.

The dog is not in cage 3.

The cat is between the hamster and the dog.

Put an **X** in the box when you know an animal does not belong in one of the cages. Put an **O** when you know an animal does belong in one of the cages. As soon as you have an O in a square, put Xs across the row and down the column.

	1	2	3	4
cat				
dog				
hamster				
rabbit				

© RBP Books   www.summerbridgeactivities.com   Reading Connection—Grade 3—RBP3829

Read and Think

1. Why is Martin taking care of the animals?
   A. It is his pet store.
   B. He is taking care of the pet store for his friend.
   C. Martin wants to buy a pet.

2. Put a **T** by the sentences that are true. Put an **F** by the sentences that are false.
   _____ The hamster belongs in cage 4.
   _____ The cat can't be in cage 1 or cage 4.
   _____ The cat is by the rabbit.
   _____ The hamster and the dog are beside each other.
   _____ Martin's friend is on vacation.

3. How did the animals get out of the cages?
   _____
   _____

4. Draw a picture of each pet in its correct cage on page 109.

Underline the three words that belong.

5. goldfish   Siamese
   turtle   crab

6. gerbil   hamster
   snake   mouse

7. cricket   tarantula
   ant   poodle

8. frog   kitten
   puppy   duckling

Word Attack

1. Write each base word.
   A. helping _____
   B. taking _____
   C. doing _____
   D. cleaning _____
   E. caring _____

To become plural, some words change their form. Some stay the same. Write the plural of the word in ( ) in the blank.

2. How many _____ can you see in the cage? (mouse)

3. There are lots of _____ near my house. (deer)

4. There is a herd of _____ in the far field. (cow)

5. We were in camp when three _____ charged between two tents. (moose)

6. The team of _____ pulled that huge slab of granite. (ox)

7. Every year that flock of _____ fly south for the winter. (goose)

8. Did you see any _____ in Yellowstone Park? (wolf)

A Hard Day's Night

Book Excerpt

1   One crisp, fall day Corinne was visiting her grandma. Grandma Cora lived down the street on the next block. Her old stucco house was painted a dark, peachy pink.

2   "Coral, that's the color," her grandma would say. "I was named after the color coral because that's the color I was when I was born. You were going to be named after me, honey bunches. You are my spittin' image. Besides, coral is the color of your hair. But your daddy wanted you to have your own name, so we settled on Corinne. See how everything in life just ties up neat and tidy!"

3   "Cora, come on! Lend me an ear," Corinne said, trying to get her grandma to listen. She always called her grandma Cora.

4   Cora had said once, "I'm not old enough to be called 'grandma.' Besides, I don't even feel like one."

5   Corinne asked her grandma if she remembered going on the camping trip down by the Potomac River the past August. The boat ride had been long, and everyone was starving when it was over. When they got back to camp, they saw Jonathan had forgotten to cover the food. Ants were all over it.

6   Jonathan was crying because Corinne said she wished he hadn't come along. Everyone was so grumpy they decided to pack up and go home. Trying to make Jonathan feel better, Aunt Margy had giggled and said she always liked aunts herself. She was one, after all.

7   All of a sudden it started to rain cats and dogs, and everything was getting wet. The dripping campers had to slog through the mud back to the car. By the time they got to Cora's jeep, sopping wet and muddy, they looked like something the cat had dragged in. Cora put in the key and turned it. Nothing happened. The battery was as dead as a doornail…

(to be continued)

www.summerbridgeactivities.com   Reading Connection—Grade 3—RBP3829

Language Skills

A **possessive pronoun** takes the place of a noun that shows belonging. Read each sentence. Write the correct pronoun from the ( ) in the space.

1. _____ hair is the color of coral. (I, my)

2. We went to visit _____ grandma down the street. (she, her)

3. Everyone knew it was _____ mistake. (his, he)

4. The fire stopped _____ laughter. (their, they)

5. Cora said to keep _____ eyes peeled. (your, you)

Word Attack

An **idiom** is a phrase that means something different than what it seems to mean. Read each phrase listed below. Then read the paragraph listed in ( ). Mark an **X** in the space by the best meaning for the phrase.

1. You are my spittin' image. (2)
   _____ I have a picture of you spitting.
   _____ We look a lot alike.
   _____ We both like to spit.

2. Lend me an ear. (3)
   _____ I would like to borrow one of your ears.
   _____ You need a hearing aid.
   _____ Would you please listen to me?

3. It started to rain cats and dogs. (7)
   _____ Cats and dogs were dropping from the sky.
   _____ It was really raining hard.
   _____ The rain sounded like dogs barking.

Fill in the dot next to the best meaning for the underlined word.

4. It was a crisp <u>fall</u> day.
   ○ autumn
   ○ to drop down to the ground
   ○ to be defeated

5. They <u>settled</u> on the best name for the baby.
   ○ to pay a bill
   ○ to sink
   ○ to agree

6. Cora will wrap the present and <u>tie</u> it with a bow.
   ○ a long piece of fabric worn knotted around a shirt collar
   ○ two teams that have the same score in a game
   ○ to join two ends of ribbon

7. Corinne asked if they could make a <u>trip</u> on the Potomac River.
   ○ to make a mistake
   ○ to stumble or fall
   ○ a journey

8. Margy hid the <u>key</u> under the mat.
   ○ one of the buttons on a computer
   ○ a piece of metal used to open a lock
   ○ a black or white bar on a piano

Book Excerpt

1   Out of the blue, Aunt Margy had started laughing and hiccuping. And they all sang "The ants go marching one by one, hurrah, hurrah. The ants go marching one by one, hurrah, hurrah. The ants go marching one by one. The little one stops to have some fun. Then they all go marching down to the ground, to get out of the rain. Boom, boom, boom, boom. Boom, boom, boom, boom."

2   "Yes, snickerdoodle, I remember," Cora said quickly. She didn't want to hear all 50 verses of that song ever again. They had sung and sung, adding more and more verses while it continued to rain. Corinne's dad, Marc, was going to come jumpstart the car. It would take three hours to get back home, with Corinne and Margy singing all the way. Cora kept chiming in—"Put a sock in it." But they kept going on and on.

3   While they were waiting for Marc, things started to get really exciting. Lightning crashed across the sky. Trees lit up, and birds screeched. With Aunt Margy hiccuping and Corinne singing about ants, Cora began to get, well, antsy. She said

they couldn't just lollygag around all night. The sound of thunder and the flash of lightning were coming closer together.

4   All of a sudden, lightning struck a tree down by the river. Aunt Margy got the hiccups scared right out of her. Corinne stopped singing. Jonathan was dead to the world and missing it all. Luckily, the downpour put out the fire. After that, they kept their eyes peeled.

5   It was then the headlights came at them— head on. They nearly jumped out of their skin. It couldn't be Marc. Cora had just called him on her cell phone…

The Ants Go Marching
The ants go marching one by one,
hurrah, hurrah!
The ants go marching one by one,
hurrah, hurrah!
The ants go marching one by one,
The little one stops to suck his thumb,
And they all go marching down to the ground,
To get out of the rain,
Boom, boom, boom, boom! Boom, boom, boom, boom!

www.summerbridgeactivities.com   Reading Connection—Grade 3—RBP3829

Read and Think

An **idiom** is a phrase that means something different than what it seems to mean.

1. List four or more idioms you can find in the story on page 113.

A. _____

_____

_____

B. _____

_____

_____

C. _____

_____

_____

D. _____

_____

_____

Word Attack

Write the word from the paragraph numbered in ( ) that has the meaning below.

1. not much (1) _____

2. the outer covering on a body (5)

_____

3. anxious (3) _____

4. to loaf or do nothing (3) _____

Try to Apply

1. Write your own verse for the song "The Ants Go Marching One by One." To keep the rhythm of the song, follow the pattern of the words in the verse on page 113.

_____

_____

_____

_____

_____

_____

_____

_____

2. Predict what might happen next in the story. Write your own ending to the chapter.

_____

_____

_____

_____

_____

_____

_____

_____

_____

Reading Connection—Grade 3—RBP3829   www.summerbridgeactivities.com   © RBP Books

It's Only a Physical Attraction

1   One of the world's greatest inventions, the magnetic compass, came from China. The first magnetic compass was made in China about 2,000 years ago.

2   Magnets come from a rock called <u>lode-stone</u>. The Chinese named the rock "loving stone" because it attracted other rocks. The Chinese used lodestones to make the first compasses.

3   The first compass had a thin iron pin. The pin was made into a magnet by rubbing it on a lodestone. Then the pin was put on top of a cork floating in a bowl of water so it could turn and point north.

4   The earth has magnetic north and south poles. So does a compass pin. The compass uses the earth's poles to work.

5   Before the compass, sailors used the sun and stars to help them sail. This method did not work in bad weather. The compass would help sailors find their way at all times.

6   But for a long time, Chinese people did not travel outside their country. They used the compass to help them decide where to put objects in homes. They did not share their ideas. The rest of the world did not get the compass for 1,000 years.

7   Try this experiment with magnetic poles: Hold one bar magnet in each hand. Try to push the ends together. If you can't do it, that means the same poles are facing each other.

8   Turn the right magnet so its other end is facing the left magnet. If the magnets stick together, that means the opposite poles are touching.

9   You have proved the saying "Opposites attract."

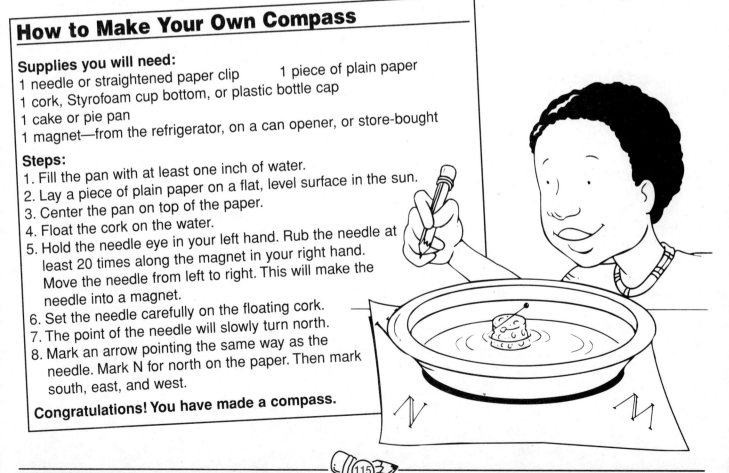

How to Make Your Own Compass

Supplies you will need:
1 needle or straightened paper clip   1 piece of plain paper
1 cork, Styrofoam cup bottom, or plastic bottle cap
1 cake or pie pan
1 magnet—from the refrigerator, on a can opener, or store-bought

Steps:
1. Fill the pan with at least one inch of water.
2. Lay a piece of plain paper on a flat, level surface in the sun.
3. Center the pan on top of the paper.
4. Float the cork on the water.
5. Hold the needle eye in your left hand. Rub the needle at least 20 times along the magnet in your right hand. Move the needle from left to right. This will make the needle into a magnet.
6. Set the needle carefully on the floating cork.
7. The point of the needle will slowly turn north.
8. Mark an arrow pointing the same way as the needle. Mark N for north on the paper. Then mark south, east, and west.

Congratulations! You have made a compass.

www.summerbridgeactivities.com   Reading Connection—Grade 3—RBP3829

Read and Think

Number the sentences in the order they happened.

1. _____ The rest of the world got the compass.

   _____ China made the first magnetic compass.

   _____ The Chinese think of a way to use the lodestone.

2. _____ Float the cork on water.

   _____ Rub the needle on a magnet.

   _____ The point of the needle will turn north.

Circle the correct answer.

3. From the story, you can tell the Chinese

   A. were very good to share.

   B. did not like to visit other countries.

   C. were romantic.

Word Attack

Write the word in the paragraph in ( ) that has the meaning below.

1. to move gently backward and forward (3) _____

2. a test (7) _____

3. to show where something is by using your finger (3) _____

Words that mean the same or nearly the same are **synonyms**. Underline the two synonyms in each row.

4. invent   paint   create   build

5. correct   write   left   right

6. bar   rod   store   lumber

7. large   small   nervous   thin

Try to Apply

Take one magnet. Look around your home for at least ten metal objects. Fill out the chart below.

Object	Attracted	Not Attracted
1.		
2.		
3.		
4.		
5.		
6.		
7.		
8.		
9.		
10.		

11. What did the objects that the magnet was attracted to have in common?

   _____

   _____

   _____

   _____

New Zealand: Home of the Kiwi

Newspaper Travel Section, Story by Nevill Strait, *Archway Sentinel*

1   Wellington, New Zealand—We were happy to see New Zealand's capital city as our plane landed. Our home in California was a long 12 hours away.

2   We saw the sea winding paths through the mountains. We had seen these fjords through the clouds.

3   The next day we took another exciting trip. Our guide drove us past extinct volcanoes. We knew active ones were not far away.

4   New Zealand has it all. We visited black sandy beaches, glaciers, and tropical rain forests. We traveled to South Island and saw one of the world's highest waterfalls. It is 1,904 feet tall. While we were sweating in the steam and heat of geysers and mud pools, our guide said it is only a 70-mile drive to the cool sea from anyplace in New Zealand. We couldn't believe it.

5   New Zealand's wildlife is the most unusual in the world. New Zealand became an island one hundred million years ago. Some of the animals did not have a chance to mix with animals from other places. That is why there are no others like them.

6   We saw a keal. The keal is a mountain parrot. It flew over our heads and landed by where we sat. Keal aren't afraid of humans. These birds have very bossy personalities.

7   Many of New Zealand's birds never travel outside their country. They are flightless. Two that we saw were the weka and the kakapo. The kakapo is the largest parrot in the world. It climbs in the shrubs and small trees.

8   The most famous of the flightless birds, however, is the kiwi. New Zealand's first settlers were the Maori. They named the bird because of its chirp, which sounds like "kiwi, kiwi, kiwi."

9   Kiwi are about the size of hens. They dig worms out of the ground with their long beaks. Their feathers are like hair. They are nocturnal, so we had to visit a kiwi house. These houses have special lights so kiwi can be seen at night.

10   Our group was confused. Someone said New Zealand's money is called "the kiwi." Another person said that people from New Zealand are nicknamed *kiwis*. Then someone else said *kiwi* was a fruit.

11   Our guide told us everyone was right. There is a picture of the kiwi on one of New Zealand's coins. New Zealanders like to be called kiwis. Then he said the kiwi fruit really came from China. But it was farmers in New Zealand that called the fruit the kiwi. They made it famous.

12   Next year we will return to go whale watching. For now, we say good-bye to the home of the kiwi.

www.summerbridgeactivities.com   Reading Connection—Grade 3—RBP3829

Read and Think

If something can be proven, it is a **fact**. If something can't be proven, it is an **opinion**. Circle **F** for fact or **O** for opinion.

1. We had seen these fjords through the clouds.
   F   O

2. New Zealand has everything you need for a great vacation.
   F   O

3. We saw the world's highest waterfall.
   F   O

4. New Zealand's wildlife is the most unusual in the world.
   F   O

5. The kakapo is the largest parrot in the world.
   F   O

Circle the correct answer.

6. From what you have read you can tell
   A. New Zealand's capital city is Wellington.
   B. the weather in New Zealand is hot.
   C. no one ever leaves New Zealand.

7. The main idea of this story is
   A. New Zealand made the kiwi famous.
   B. The birds in New Zealand are unusual.
   C. New Zealand is a land of variety.

Word Attack

Circle the correct answer.

1. From what you have read, you can tell the word <u>fjord</u> (2) means
   A. a dream.
   B. a mountain window.
   C. an inlet cut into the mountains by the sea.

2. The word <u>kiwi</u> means all of the following except
   A. a small flightless bird.
   B. a Chinese immigrant.
   C. a fruit.

Language Skills

A word that describes something is an **adjective**. Read each sentence. Circle the adjective. Underline the word it describes.

1. We took an exciting trip.

2. We stood beside the muddy pools.

3. We visited black beaches.

4. At night we visited a kiwi house.

5. Keal have bossy personalities.

A Migration Invitation

Wheeler Elementary Weekly, by Brynne Eskelson, Reporter

Wheeler Elementary Bears
Weekly Newsletter

You can travel by boat to go whale watching, or you can wait for whales to come to you. You would be lucky if you lived in Japan, Hawaii, or Mexico. Once a year the Northern Pacific humpback whales travel to these countries from Alaska. They have their babies in the warm, shallow waters near the coasts.

The trip the whales make is called a <u>migration</u>. Humpback whales begin their summer feeding near Alaska. They feed from June to October. By November they stop eating. Now the whales are ready to migrate 3,500 miles to winter homes.

Some whales can travel the long distance in 39 days. Try this to figure out how many miles a day one humpback whale can travel. Divide 3,500 miles by 39 days. Divide your first answer by 12. That is how many miles an hour the whale can swim.

Did you know that each whale's flukes are unique? A fluke is a tail fin, and it is like the whale's fingerprint. No two are alike. This makes it easier to keep track of individual whales. Scientists found out how fast the humpback whales could migrate by checking the flukes.

Humpback whales are as curious as cats. They will come right up to a boat of people whale watching. People can see the whales doing tricks when they come to the surface to breathe. It is called "spy-hopping" if the whale lifts one third of its body out of the water. If it slaps the water with its tail, it is called "lobtailing."

Everyone's favorite trick is when a whale "breeches." Its entire body, 40 feet long and weighing 30 tons, comes up out of the water. Then it crashes back down with a giant belly flop. The noise is like thunder in the sky.

Humpback whales make the best noise when they sing. Of course, they can't sing like people do. They have no vocal cords, and no air is blown out. No one knows for sure how they sing. Some scientists think air circles around inside tubes in the whales' bodies to make the noise.

One song can last for 20 minutes. People recorded some of the songs and made an album. It was a big hit at music stores. Remember the humpback whale next time you travel. Its song might invite you to join the migration. Maybe you can travel along.

Read and Think

Circle **T** if the sentence is true. Circle **F** if the sentence is false.

1. You can see the humpback whale if you live in Japan, Hawaii, or Italy.
   T   F

2. The trip the whales make is called a migration.
   T   F

3. A humpback whale gives birth in the waters around Alaska.
   T   F

4. Some whales can travel from Alaska to Hawaii in 39 days.
   T   F

5. A whale is lobtailing if it slaps the water with its head.
   T   F

Number the sentences in the order they happen.

6. _____ Some whales travel the long distance in 39 days.

   _____ By November they stop eating.

   _____ The humpback whales feed from June to October.

   _____ They have their babies in the warm, shallow waters near the coasts.

Language Skills

Some words, like *I, she, he, we, it,* and *they,* are used in place of other words. They are called **pronouns**. Read each sentence. Fill in the blank.

1. Once a year, humpback whales travel to Mexico. They have babies near the coast.

   <u>They</u> stands for _____.

2. People can see the whales doing tricks when they come to the surface.

   <u>They</u> stands for _____.

3. People recorded some of the songs and made an album. It was a big hit.

   <u>It</u> stands for _____.

Try to Apply

List five facts you have read about humpback whales. Use these facts to help you make up names for five whales.

	Facts	**Names**
1.	_____	_____
2.	_____	_____
3.	_____	_____
4.	_____	_____
5.	_____	_____

A Kiwi Treat

From *Children Can Cook in Many Countries Cookbook*

New Zealand's Pavlova

Ingredients:

$\frac{1}{2}$ tsp. salt

$\frac{3}{4}$ tsp. vanilla

$\frac{3}{4}$ c. caster sugar*

3 egg whites

$\frac{1}{4}$ tsp. cream of tartar

* Caster sugar is a very fine sugar from New Zealand.
You can find it in specialty shops. Powdered sugar
may be substituted.

Equipment:

1 baking sheet

1 small mixing bowl

1 wooden spoon

1 egg separator

1 airtight container

measuring cups

wax paper

measuring spoons

electric mixer

- Assemble the ingredients.
- Lay out the equipment.
- Preheat the oven to 300 degrees.

1. Set the egg separator over the bowl. Carefully crack one egg into the separator. The egg yolk will stay in the separator. The egg white will fall into the bowl. Crack two more eggs in the same way.

2. Set the egg whites aside at room temperature for one half hour. Save the egg yolks in a container to use another time. Put them in the refrigerator.

3. Tear off a sheet of wax paper the same size as the baking sheet. Draw 12 three-inch circles onto the wax paper. An easy way to do this is to use a compass. From the center point, measure out $1\frac{1}{2}$ inches. That should give you a three-inch circle. Turn the wax paper so the writing side is down. Place the paper on the baking sheet.

4. Add vanilla, cream of tartar, and salt to the egg whites. Beat with an electric mixer on high speed. Do this until soft peaks form. Make sure to have an adult help you.

5. Add sugar one tablespoon at a time. Keep beating at high speed until stiff peaks form. The sugar should be almost dissolved. This takes about five minutes. You have just made <u>meringue</u>.

6. Put equal spoonfuls of meringue onto each circle. Use all of the mixture. Build up the sides to make bowls.

7. Bake in the oven for 35 minutes. Then turn off the oven and let the bowls dry for one hour. Carefully pull each bowl off the wax paper. Store them in an airtight container.

Filling:

Pile any fresh fruit, such as peaches or strawberries, into the shell. Top with dairy whipped topping from a container. Drizzle a little bottled fruit sauce on top.

Read and Think

Cause is why something happens. **Effect** is what happens after. Circle the correct cause.

1. The egg white will fall into the bowl
   A. when it gets to room temperature.
   B. if no one catches it.
   C. if you crack the egg over the egg separator.

2. Stiff peaks will form
   A. when the cook gets angry.
   B. when you have beaten the egg whites long enough.
   C. if the room is cold.

3. The meringue bowls will not stick to the baking sheet
   A. when you put down wax paper.
   B. if they are pulled off fast enough.
   C. because there is no glue in the recipe.

Study Hall

A **glossary** gives the meaning of special words or phrases used in a book.

---

c.= cup (kuhp) 1. noun A cup measure or eight ounces of an ingredient.

cream of tartar (kreem uhv tartur) 1. noun A salt found in the spice section of the grocery store.

drizzle (driz-uhl) 1. verb To lightly sprinkle with a liquid topping.

ingredient (in-gree-dee-uhnt) 1. noun An item of food used in a recipe.

meringue (muh-rang) 1. noun A baked mixture of sugar and stiffly beaten egg whites.

preheat (pree-heet) 1. verb To heat an oven ahead of time.

soft peak (sawft peek) 1. noun A high point that curves to one side.

stiff peak (stif peek) 1. noun A high point that is not bent over.

tsp.= teaspoon (tee-spoon) 1. noun A small spoon used to measure an ingredient.

Use this Cooking Terms Glossary to answer the questions below. If the underlined word in the sentence means the same as the word in the glossary, write **Yes** in the blank. Write **No** if it does not mean the same.

1. David tried to <u>cup</u> his hand around the flame to stop the wind from blowing out the fire. _____

2. The early morning <u>drizzle</u> had left everything smelling fresh. _____

3. Marta was missing a key <u>ingredient</u> for her shepherd's pie. _____

Write the correct word for the meaning on the line.

4. To heat an oven before you are ready to bake. _____

5. The top of a beaten mixture that looks like a mountain top gently curving to one side.

   _____

6. A salt found in the grocery store. _____

7. Number these steps in the order they should be done.

   _____ Save the egg yolks in a container to use another time.

   _____ Carefully pull each bowl off the wax paper.

   _____ Build up the sides to make the bowls.

   _____ Beat with an electric mixer on high speed.

   _____ Pile any fresh fruit into the shell.

   _____ Set the egg whites aside for one half hour.

"A Challenge to Others"

Interview

Reporter: This is Mavis Berk from WING radio. I am with Amelia Earhart in Miami, Florida. It is June 1, 1937. May I ask you some questions, Amelia?

Amelia: Yes, I have some time. They are getting the plane ready for our trip.

Reporter: Amelia, how did you feel when you saw a plane for the first time?

Amelia: I was at the Iowa State Fair. The plane I saw was made of wire and wood. It was not very exciting. I rode in a plane for the first time when I was about 20.

Reporter: Where did you live then?

Amelia: We were living in California, and our family was at an airplane show. It was there that I flew for the very first time. The ride lasted only ten minutes, but I knew I wanted to learn to fly.

Reporter: When did you meet your husband, George Putnam?

Amelia: George was a New York publisher when we met. He asked me to be the first woman to fly across the Atlantic Ocean.

Reporter: Were you alone when you flew that time in 1928?

Amelia: Oh, no! I was not even flying the plane. I just rode along for that trip.

Reporter: Let's travel back to 1932. What happened in May of that year?

Amelia: I am always looking for exciting things to do. Charles Lindberg had flown solo across the Atlantic. That was something no one else had done. So on

May 20, 1932, I began the flight alone from Canada to England.

Reporter: But your plane landed in a pasture in Ireland.

Amelia: Yes, the plane had flown a little off course. There was a man in the field watching the plane. He asked me if I had come a long way. I told him I had come from America. I had achieved George's goal.

Reporter: You are also the only person to fly across the Atlantic Ocean two times. President Roosevelt said you have shown that women can fly as well as men. Do you think you can set another record?

Amelia: It will be a challenge. Fred Noonan and I are planning to fly around the world. Fred will decide where we fly. He's my navigator.

Reporter: Good luck, Amelia! Have a safe trip.

Amelia: Thank you, Mavis.

On June 1, 1937, everything was ready. Amelia and Fred Noonan left Florida flying the *Electra*. They were going to fly around the world.

On June 29 the plane was in New Guinea. They had flown 22,000 miles! Amelia and Fred only had 7,000 miles to go. But the whole trip was over the Pacific Ocean. July 2 was the last time anyone heard from them.

President Roosevelt asked for ships and planes to search the ocean. They searched for 16 days. They never found the two fliers.

Amelia had written a letter to George. In it she wrote, "Women must try to do things as men have tried. When they fail, their failure must be a challenge to others."

Read and Think

1. The main idea of the interview is _____.
   A. flying is dangerous
   B. always fly with a buddy
   C. a person's failures should be a challenge to others

2. Number the sentences in the order they happened.

   _____ Amelia and Fred had 7,000 miles to go.

   _____ She saw her first plane at the Iowa State Fair.

   _____ There was a man in the field watching the plane.

   _____ Amelia and Fred leave to fly around the world.

3. Write **T** if the statement is true. Write **F** if the statement is false.

   _____ The first plane Amelia saw was made of wood and tape.

   _____ Amelia knew she wanted to fly when she went to school.

   _____ On June 29, 1931, Amelia Earhart left to fly alone across the Atlantic Ocean.

   _____ Amelia became the only person at that time to fly across the Atlantic two times.

Study Hall

Use the Table of Contents to answer the questions below.

Fantastic Flight

Table of Contents

1. In what chapter would you find out about Charles Lindbergh? _____

2. What is chapter five titled? _____

3. On what page does chapter three start?

   _____

4. On what page would you find out about the history of airplanes? _____

5. Which chapter would tell you how an airplane's wings worked? _____

Mind Buster

People have many ideas about what might have happened to Amelia Earhart and Fred Noonan. Write three sentences telling what you think. Did they die? Were they stranded on a deserted island? Use your imagination.

_____

_____

_____

Mistaken Identity

Jewish Folktale

1   Once, a rabbi was traveling with his devoted students. It had been a long day. It was decided by all that they should stop. They found an inn where they could sleep for the night.

2   This inn was a popular stopping place for travelers and was quite crowded. However, the innkeeper was hoping to please the rabbi. That was how the rabbi and his seven companions came to take the room at the back.

3   Such a room! It was quiet and very dark because there were no windows. The rabbi took the only bed—it was lumpy. His students scattered their mats on the floor around him.

4   It was a misfortune in the end. But who was to know it would happen? One student had to take an early train back into the city, so he slept close to the door. It would be easier to answer the call to wake.

5   The innkeeper rapped softly at the door in the early morning hours. The student did not want to disturb his fellows, so he felt around for his clothes in the pitch black.

6   It was a mistake that he put the rabbi's long, black gown on. Hurrying quickly down the cold lonely streets, he had but one worry—that he might miss his train. He wrapped the cloak tightly around him against the cold and took no notice of what he wore.

7   As he entered the station house he stood amazed. Turning from side to side in front of the lobby mirror, he became angry. He turned away from the smirks of those around him.

8   "What is this!" he exclaimed. Trying to hide his dismay, he faced the mirror again. "It is true, that fool of an innkeeper! I asked that he wake me, and instead he woke the rabbi. Now I have slept in and shall be late for my train!"

    www.summerbridgeactivities.com   **Reading Connection—Grade 3—RBP3829**

Read and Think

1. In paragraph 4, "It was a misfortune" probably means _____.
   A. it is not safe to sleep on the floor
   B. the dark room was the cause of the mistake
   C. the fortuneteller was wrong

Cause is why something happens. **Effect** is what takes place afterward. Circle the correct cause.

2. The rabbi and students took a room at the back because
   A. they were not important.
   B. the innkeeper was not nice to them.
   C. they were tired, and it would be dark and quiet.

3. The student put on the rabbi's robe because
   A. it was handy.
   B. he wanted to be a rabbi.
   C. it was dark and he couldn't see.

4. The student thinks he is the rabbi because
   A. he is dreaming.
   B. he is dressed like him.
   C. the mirror is magic.

Word Attack

Homophones are words that sound the same but are spelled differently and mean different things. Read each word. Look for its homophone in the paragraph shown in ( ). Write the word in the blank.

1. awl (1) _____
2. in (1) _____
3. four (2) _____
4. know (3) _____
5. won (4) _____
6. rapped (6) _____
7. sighed (7) _____
8. bee (8) _____
9. wood (4) _____

Study Hall

Make a check by each word that could be found between these dictionary guide words.

1. decoration/elegant
   ____ devoted
   ____ day
   ____ door
   ____ decided

2. macaroni/mislead
   ____ misfortune
   ____ mats
   ____ mistake
   ____ mirror

3. salad/sticky
   ____ stopping
   ____ scattered
   ____ sleep
   ____ station

4. rapid/silk
   ____ softly
   ____ rabbi
   ____ rapped
   ____ smirks

Language Skills

A **main verb** is the most important verb in a sentence. It shows action. A **helping verb** joins together with the main verb. Forms of *be* and *have* are helping verbs. Circle the helping verb. Underline the main verb.

1. Once a rabbi was traveling.
2. His students had scattered the mats on the floor.
3. The student was hurrying.
4. I have slept late this morning!

Animals Travel

The Turtle

When traveling far it becomes quite a hurdle,
Deciding where you will sleep.
But when you're a turtle with a shell for a girdle,
Your hotel room comes quite cheap.

Kangaroo

Have you ever gone for a
    kangaroo ride,
With the driver on the out and
    the passengers inside?
Well, the trip I'm here to tell you,
    leaves a lot to be desired,
With hopping all about, the tires
    need retired.

Not to mention there's no seats,
And you're hanging on for life,
Plus the lighting is quite dark,
No more of kangarooing strife
                    —for me!

Roadrunner

Roadrunner is quite different—
He likes to take a tan,
When running on hot dessert roads
I think I'd need a fan.

His cuckoo family members fly,
But Runner hits the road.
I don't know who is "cuckier,"
Or what's the better mode.

The Ostrich Is a Silly Bird

The ostrich is a silly bird,
    With scarcely any mind,
He often runs so very fast,
    He leaves himself behind.

And when he gets there has to stand
    And hang about till night,
Without a blessed thing to do
    Until he comes in sight.

Mary E. Wilkins Freeman

Elephant

The elephant carries a great big trunk,
He never packs it with clothes.
It has no lock, and it has no key,
So he takes it wherever he goes.

Anonymous

127

Read and Think

Circle the correct answer.

1. In "The Turtle," "Your hotel room comes quite cheap" probably means
   A. turtles have no money.
   B. a turtle sleeps for free in its shell.
   C. rooms for turtles cost less.

2. In the poem "Kangaroo," you can tell a kangaroo ride is
   A. quite peaceful.
   B. uncomfortable.
   C. lonely.

3. In the poem "Elephant," you can tell an elephant's trunk
   A. opens with a combination.
   B. stays with him all the time.
   C. holds a lot of stuff.

4. In the poem "Roadrunner," "hits the road" probably means
   A. falls down a lot.
   B. likes to run on the road instead of fly.
   C. is not nice to the road.

5. In the poem "The Ostrich Is a Silly Bird," the ostrich is waiting for
   A. himself.
   B. someone to give him a ride.
   C. his older brother.

6. Which three animals provide the wildest ride in the poems? Circle the correct answer.
   A. turtle, roadrunner, and elephant
   B. turtle, ostrich, and roadrunner
   C. ostrich, kangaroo, and roadrunner

Language Skills

Underline the three words that belong.

1. turtle   elephant
   ostrich   kangaroo

2. hopping   sleeping
   running   traveling

3. seat   trunk
   tires   driver

Synonyms are words that have similar meanings. Find a word in the poem in ( ) that means the same as the word listed.

4. nap ("The Turtle")_____

5. journey ("Kangaroo") _____

6. large ("Elephant")_____

7. brain ("The Ostrich Is a Silly Bird") _____

Try to Apply

What kind of animal would you want to be if you were going to travel?

_____

_____

_____

_____

Reading Connection—Grade 3—RBP3829   www.summerbridgeactivities.com   ©RBP Books

Eight Minutes Over France

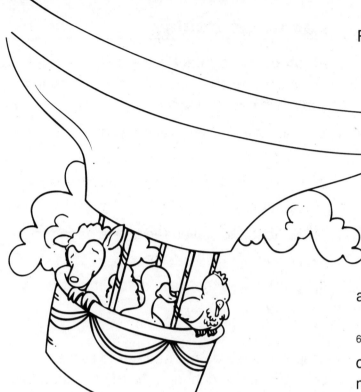

1   Do you like to travel in different ways? Then try going by hot air balloon. The idea had been around for 2,000 years. But it took the king of France, two brothers, a sheep, a duck, and a chicken to make it happen.

2   The king of France thought a man would die up in a balloon. So, two brothers did a test. They sent up the three animals in a basket attached to a balloon.

3   The animals flew over France for eight minutes. The king was excited when they returned safely. Two months later, a major in the army and a physics professor went up in a balloon.

4   A hot air balloon is so simple, anyone could fly one. Just turn a knob to let gas into the balloon. This makes the balloon go up.

Pulling a cord makes the balloon rise quickly or slowly. If the cord lets enough gas out, the balloon will sink. The wind moves the balloon from place to place.

5   In the 1960s, hot air balloons became very popular. Ed Yost and Raven Industries began to design and make hot air balloons. Then the United States Navy asked Ed's company to help them. The Navy wanted to use balloons to send packages.

6   Ed Yost and the Navy made important changes. Balloons were made from a new material. The balloon's shape was made to look like a giant lightbulb.

7   Someone also thought of a new way to inflate the balloon. Now they just fill the top part of the balloon. Some safety changes were also made. It is safer than ever to travel by hot air balloon.

8   After a while, the Navy lost interest in hot air balloons. But Ed Yost didn't give up. He sold hot air balloons for sports events.

9   Hot air balloon businesses make millions of dollars. Balloon races attract crowds of watchers. Many people take part in the fun.

10   Everyone should ride in a hot air balloon! Some people travel around the world in one. Once you have tried it, you will never want to fly any other way.

Read and Think

If something can be proven, it is a **fact**. If something can't be proven, it is an **opinion**. Circle **F** for fact or **O** for opinion.

1. The king was excited when they returned safely. (3)

   F   O

2. A hot air balloon is so simple, anyone can fly one. (4)

   F   O

3. It is safer than ever to travel by hot air balloon. (7)

   F   O

4. Everyone should ride in a hot air balloon. (10)

   F   O

5. Once you have tried it, you will never want to fly any other way. (10)

   F   O

You can often tell what a word means by looking at the words around it. Read the paragraph in ( ). Circle the correct answer.

6. The word sink (4) means

   A. to go toward the ground.

   B. to rise up slowly.

   C. a place to wash your hands.

7. The word inflate (7) means

   A. a new idea.

   B. to fill something up with air.

   C. a safety change.

Language Skills

A **compound subject** is two or more nouns connected by *and*. Underline the compound subject in each sentence.

1. The king of France and two brothers made it happen.

2. A major in the army and a physics professor went up.

3. Ed Yost and Raven Industries began to design hot air balloons.

4. Ed Yost and the Navy made important changes.

Irregular verbs do not add **-ed** to make the past tense. They change their form. Read each sentence. Write the present tense of the underlined verb in the blank.

5. The king of France thought a man would die up in a balloon. _____

6. So, two brothers did a test. _____

7. Ed Yost and Raven Industries began to design hot air balloons. _____

8. The Navy lost interest. _____

9. He sold hot air balloons for sports events.

   _____

Mind Buster!

Why do you think an army major and a physics professor were the two men chosen to go up in the balloon?

_____

_____

_____

Reading Connection—Grade 3—RBP3829   www.summerbridgeactivities.com   © RBP Books

The Incredible Incredible Journey

By Peter Troy, *Mount Olivet Elementary Sentinel*

Have you ever run away from home?

Do you like traveling? Do you like animals? Do you like happy endings? Then read *The Incredible Journey* by Sheila Burnford. Reading it is an incredible journey.

The story is about three animals that run away to return home. They have been staying with a friend while their owners are gone. Then the friend decides to take a vacation. The housekeeper is going to watch the pets for a few days.

That is one too many changes for the pets. The golden lab, bulldog, and Siamese cat miss their owners. So they decide to head for home. Their incredible journey begins.

If you haven't read the book, maybe you have seen the movie *Homeward Bound: The Incredible Journey*. There are things that are different about the book and the movie. There are also many things they have in common. The big difference is that the animals talk in their minds in the movie. The author tells what happens in the book.

In the movie, the pets' names are Shadow, Chance, and Sassy, the only girl. In the book, the lab's name is Luath, the old bulldog is Bodger, and the cat is Tao. All three of the pets are male.

In one part of the book, Luath gets his nose stung by a porcupine. A nice family finds him and helps remove the porcupine quills. But it is Chance whose nose gets hurt in the movie. A dogcatcher picks him up and takes him to the vet to get well.

My favorite part is the same in both the movie and the book, the ending. The ending is a little different if you've watched it. But both endings will still make you feel the same. You will yell, clap, and dance.

After you read the book, you will know how your pet feels when it is left alone. Sheila Burnford writes so you imagine you are along on the journey. By the end, you'll feel like these pets are yours. It's an incredible feeling.

www.summerbridgeactivities.com   **Reading Connection—Grade 3—RBP3829**

Read and Think

Circle the correct answer.

1. The main idea of this book review is
   A. a pet gets lonely when you leave to go somewhere.
   B. the book and the movie are different.
   C. reading *The Incredible Journey* is a great experience.

2. Three things that are different about the book and the movie are
   A. the names of the animals, talking animals, and which animal gets stung by a porcupine.
   B. the names of the animals, which animal is older, and where the animals are going.
   C. talking animals, how many animals are male, and where the animals are going.

Circle **F** for fact or **O** for opinion.

3. That is one too many changes for the pets.
   F   O

4. The big difference is that animals talk.
   F   O

5. Both endings will make you feel the same.
   F   O

6. After you read the book, you will know how your pet feels.
   F   O

Language Skills

A **possessive pronoun** shows ownership or belonging. It takes the place of a noun that shows ownership or belonging. Some possessive pronouns are *my, your, his, her, its, our,* and *their.* Underline the possessive pronoun in the sentence, and write the noun it stands for.

1. The animals are staying with a friend while their owners are away.
   _____

2. Sassy is traveling with her friends.
   _____

3. Luath gets his nose stung by a porcupine.
   _____

4. Peter said, "My favorite part is the end."
   _____

Word Attack

Sometimes an *'s* is used to show ownership or belonging. Add *'s* to each word below, and write the correct word in the blank.

book   **pet**

friend   **lab**

1. owners _____

2. vacation _____

3. nose _____

4. ending _____

A Most Excellent Adventure

San Carlos Morning News

Have you ever lost a pet?

Morning News

1   SAN CARLOS, Calif. (WP)— Today Ted, a pet that likes to travel, is safe and back at home. Ted is a black cat who has had some bad luck. Ten years ago he jumped out of a window and was gone.

2   He had begun a most excellent adventure. The cat was named after Ted in the movie *Bill and Ted's Excellent Adventure.* No one is sure where Ted was or why he left. Chris Inglis, Ted's owner, said Ted had seemed content and happy. Ted's sleek black coat looked good. The cat seemed to have been fed and taken care of while he was gone.

3   In the 1990s someone came up with the idea to put a microchip under an animal's skin. When people found a lost pet they could take it to a shelter to have it checked. Then the owner could come and pick up the pet.

4   Ted had a chip, but it was ten years before someone found Ted and took him to an animal shelter. He was thirteen miles from his old home. People at the shelter said it took a little time to find Chris Inglis. The address and phone number on the chip were incorrect. Chris said he couldn't believe it when the shelter called and said they had Ted.

5   Ted seemed to be the same, even after ten years of travel. Chris said Ted "rubbed his face on my hand, climbed right up, and started purring." One of the things the two of them liked to do was ride around town in Chris's car. On the way home from the shelter, Chris said Ted "put his front paws on the dashboard," just like he used to. Ted the cat felt right at home.

© RBP Books   www.summerbridgeactivities.com   Reading Connection—Grade 3—RBP3829

Read and Think

Circle the correct answer.

1. Ted had bad luck because
   A. he was black.
   B. he jumped out of a window and was lost.
   C. he didn't have a place to live.

2. Ted's owner got his cat back because
   A. he called him.
   B. someone took care of Ted.
   C. he had a microchip put under Ted's skin.

3. The main idea of this newspaper article is
   A. cats run away all the time.
   B. black cats are unlucky.
   C. a microchip helped return Ted to his owner.

Word Attack

The prefixes **in-, un-,** and **dis-** mean "not." Write the correct prefix in the blank. One of the words has two answers.

in	un	dis

_____ correct   _____ content
_____ lucky   _____ happy
_____ belief   _____ safe
_____ direct   _____ believable

Language Skills

A **main verb** is the most important verb in a sentence. It shows action. A **helping verb** joins together with the main verb. Forms of the verbs *be* and *have* are helping verbs.

is	**was**	**were**
has	**had**	

Write the correct helping verb in the blank.

1. The people at the shelter _____ surprised to find the chip.

2. Ted _____ gone for ten years.

3. The black cat _____ traveled thirteen miles.

4. Christ Inglis _____ his pet home now.

5. Ted _____ glad to be back.

Adjectives are words that tell about something. Read each adjective. The paragraph you will find it in is in ( ). Find the word the adjective tells about and write it in the blank.

6. black (1) _____   9. thirteen (4) _____
7. front (5)_____   10. lost (3) _____
8. old (4) _____   11. animal (4) _____

Mind Buster

Write your own ad for a pet you might have found. Remember, newspaper columns are narrow, and you are charged $4 for every line. You do not have to write complete sentences, but you do have to write all the important information.

_____
_____
_____

Out of This World

Would you like to be an astronaut when you grow up?

1   One way to travel is by spaceship. A spaceship can take you out of this world to places no one has gone. By 1970, Americans were used to people going into space. Space travel was normal and safe.

2   On April 13, 1970, things changed quickly. Part of the *Apollo 13* spaceship exploded. The crew on the ship was more than halfway to the moon.

3   That day they had been doing their normal jobs. One of the astronauts flipped a switch that mixed up oxygen in tanks that were next to the spaceship. No one knew that some of the wiring was bad. While the mixing was going on, a spark was created. That set the oxygen on fire.

4   All at once, several bad things happened. The spaceship's electrical and operating systems were gone. The crew's oxygen was escaping. There was no chance of them landing on the moon. There was even a chance the astronauts might not make it back to earth.

5   The crew could not stay in the part of the spaceship where they were. They had to move into the part that would have landed on the moon. There they could stay alive for a while. But no one knew if there was enough air and water to stay alive on the trip home. That part of the ship was only made for two people.

6   To help the astronauts get home safely, the temperature in the cabin where they stayed was kept close to freezing. That helped them save power. They could only have six ounces of water each day. It was going to be a close call.

7   Instead of turning around toward the earth, the spaceship was still going to the moon. This turned out to be a smart move. The astronauts used the gravity of the moon to push their spaceship back to the earth. The crew made it home by the skin of their teeth.

8   Everyone called the flight a success. The scientists had learned a lot about accidents in space and how to take care of them from earth. Also, everyone on board the ship came home alive!

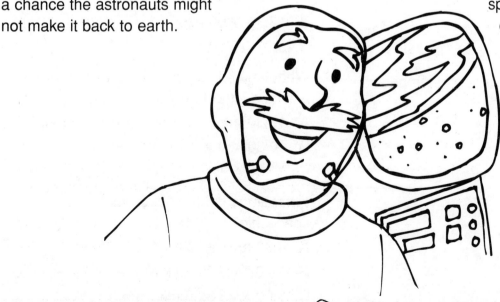

© RBP Books   www.summerbridgeactivities.com   Reading Connection—Grade 3—RBP3829

Read and Think

Circle the correct answer.

1. The main idea of the passage is
   A. people should not go up in space.
   B. space travel is risky.
   C. scientists learn a lot when astronauts travel in space.

2. In paragraph 7, "by the skin of their teeth" probably means
   A. skin grows on teeth in space.
   B. they were lucky to make it home.
   C. the astronauts lost a lot of weight.

3. The title "Out of This World" probably refers to
   A. exciting space travel.
   B. aliens traveling in space.
   C. the high price of space travel being out of reach for most people.

4. Number these events in the order they happened.
   ____ The astronauts arrive home safely.
   ____ Oxygen was escaping from the ship.
   ____ The astronauts moved into a different part of the ship.
   ____ The oxygen caught fire.
   ____ The oxygen was being mixed.
   ____ The scientists lowered the temperature.
   ____ A spark was created.

Mind Buster

Read about space travel. List the flights on which astronauts have died and the dates.

Study Hall

Read the astronauts' schedule. Then answer the questions.

8:00 A.M.	Wake up / Get dressed
8:20	Talk to mission control
8:30	Eat breakfast / Visit with each other
9:00	Housekeeping / Experiments Ship maintenance
11:00	Exercise
12:30 P.M.	Lunch
2:00	Experiments / Ship maintenance
4:30	Short break
4:45	Work
7:30	Dinner
8:30	Housekeeping
9:30	Short break
10:00	Talk to mission control
10:10	Personal time
Midnight	Lights out

1. The astronauts talked with mission control for _____ each time.
   A. 1 hour
   B. long periods
   C. 10 minutes

2. When might an astronaut check on the plant-growing experiments?
   A. 9:00–10:00 A.M.
   B. 12:30–2:00 P.M.
   C. 9:30–10:00 P.M.

3. What time could you find an astronaut writing a letter home?
   A. 10:30 P.M.
   B. 10:30 A.M.
   C. 11:00 A.M.

4. What times did the astronauts clean the spaceship?
   A. 4:30 P.M., 9:30 P.M.
   B. 10:00 A.M., 8:30 P.M.
   C. 9:00 A.M., 8:30 P.M.

Class Journal Entry

October 1, 1999

What would you do if you were the only person left on earth?

1   Do you know what a tragedy is? It is something very sad that happens. In 1914, a tragedy occurred. Martha, the last passenger pigeon, died.

2   Today, Tess Wright came to our class. She talked about pigeons and brought a dove for us to see. She said the dove looked a lot like the passenger pigeon. Tess showed us a picture of Martha and a male bird.

3   Martha was not that pretty, but the male bird was. Its body was gray with black streaks. Its chest was a rose color. Its throat was pink, shiny brown, green, and purple.

4   One time, a while ago, there were five billion of these birds. Wow! When a flock flew by, there were so many birds the sky got dark. It took hours for them to fly past.

5   But something happened. By 1905 no one could find any of these wild pigeons. A reward was offered for a nest, but no one could find one.

6   Miss Wright said there is safety in numbers. Passenger pigeons lived in large groups, so enemies like the wolf or fox couldn't eat all of them. There were always more birds.

7   But staying together made them weak against another enemy: humans. One man could kill a lot of birds quickly. At one time, 12 dead birds sold for 50 cents.

8   People didn't keep good records on birds at that time. No one knew how many pigeons were left. Then all of the birds were gone.

9   Tess asked our class to vote. Who thought that people had killed all the passenger pigeons? We all raised our hands. We were partly wrong. Hunters were one of the reasons the pigeons were gone. But people also cut down the forests where the birds nested. Then they made farms on the land. The birds had no place to make a home. Soon there were no more baby pigeons.

    The Smithsonian Museum has Martha now. Near her body is a sign that says:

Last of her species, died at 1 P.M., 1 September 1914, age 29, in the Cincinnati Zoological Garden

EXTINCT

    Miss Wright gave each of us a card to remind us about passenger pigeons. Something good happened when Martha died. People made laws to protect birds. I think Martha would have liked that.

Read and Think

Circle the correct answer.

1. It took hours for the birds to fly past because
   A. they couldn't see in the dark.
   B. the trees were in the way.
   C. there were a lot of them.

2. From what you have read in paragraph 6 you can tell "safety in numbers" means
   A. the passenger pigeon knew math.
   B. the pigeons' great numbers protected them from becoming extinct.
   C. all pigeons knew the safety rules.

3. Number the events in the order they happened.
   _____ The passenger pigeon became extinct.
   _____ There were five billion passenger pigeons.
   _____ People cut down the forests.
   _____ They farmed the land.
   _____ There were no baby pigeons.

Word Attack

Homophones are words that sound the same but are spelled differently and mean different things. Underline the correct word.

1. The sky got dark when the birds_____by. (flu, flew)

2. _____ of the passenger pigeons are gone. (Awl, All)

3. They were too _____ to survive their enemies. (weak, week)

Study Hall

Use the dictionary entry to answer the questions.

trag e dy (traj-uh-dee), n. 1. A play with a sad ending. 2. A very sad event. noun, plural tragedies

1. Underline the sentence in which tragedy means the same as definition number two.

   We saw the tragedy *Romeo and Juliet* at the Hale Center Playhouse.

   It was a tragedy that so many people died on September 11, 2001.

Circle the correct answer.

2. The word tragedy is
   A. an adjective.
   B. a noun.
   C. a verb.

3. Tragedy has _____ syllables.
   A. three
   B. four
   C. two

Language Skills

Rewrite the sentences below in the correct order. Remember to start each sentence with a capital letter and end each with the correct punctuation.

1. visitor our had a class
   _____

2. extinct passenger is the why pigeon
   _____

3. was there no to place build left a nest
   _____

Bill and Ted's Excellent Adventure: Party On, Dudes!

By Trista Simpson, Ranger Plains Elementary   Movie Review

1   *Bill and Ted's Excellent Adventure* is so totally excellent! Alex Winter is Bill, and Keanu Reeves is Ted. They are teenagers from San Dimas, California. Their goal in life is to become famous rock stars.

2   These two are flunking their history class. Plus, they have a major project due tomorrow! It could not be worse. Wait, it could be. Ted's father will send him to military school in Alaska if Ted flunks.

3   Out of the blue pops a phone booth with George Carlin inside. He is Rufus, a special agent from the future. The future does not look good if these guys don't pass history. They will be torn apart, and Ted will be sent to Alaska. If this happens, they won't be able to sing in their band, Wyld Stallyns.

4   Rufus has been sent to help the boys with their history project. He tells them to get in the phone booth and hold on tight. Then Bill, Ted, and Rufus travel through time. It is fun to see them pick up different famous people along the way. Napoleon, Genghis Khan, Socrates (Sew Crates), and more crowd into the phone booth. Back they go to the future.

5   Then the real adventure begins. Napoleon has a power struggle over a water park. Sew Crates becomes an expert on soap operas. Genghis Khan wrecks a sports store. You will laugh your head off as you watch these guys.

6   Will Bill and Ted pass history? Will the future be saved? Will all the famous people want to stay in the future? Watch to find out. You will never see a better movie—not in a million years.

Read and Think

Circle **F** if the sentence is a fact or **O** if it is an opinion.

1. Back they go to the future. (4)

   F   O

2. You will never see a better movie. (6)

   F   O

3. It could not be worse. (2)

   F   O

4. Watch to find out. (6)

   F   O

5. Genghis Khan wrecks a sports store. (5)

   F   O

An **idiom** is a phrase that means something different than what the words seem to say. Read each phrase below. Then read the paragraph listed in ( ). Mark an **X** by the best meaning for the phrase.

6. Out of the blue pops a phone booth. (3)

   _____ The phone booth is behind a blue door.

   _____ The phone booth was floating.

   _____ Suddenly, a phone booth appears.

7. They will be torn apart. (3)

   _____ Bill's dad will tear off their legs.

   _____ The boys will be in different places.

   _____ They will feel like a piece of paper.

8. You will laugh your head off. (5)

   _____ It will be really funny.

   _____ You'll laugh so hard your head will fall off your neck.

   _____ Your head makes you laugh.

Try to Apply

Read the movie schedule. Then answer the questions below.

```
┌─────────────────────────────────────────┐
│         Barker's Cinema Theatre          │
│    8560 Trenton Way (053) 712-3305       │
│                                          │
│      $7.50 ADULTS FRI. & SAT.            │
│      $7.00 ADULTS SUN.-THURS.            │
│   $4.75 CHILD & MATINEES BEFORE 6 P.M.   │
│        Bargain Shows in ( )              │
│          THE ROOKIE (G)                  │
│       (12:15  2:20  4:20) 6:15           │
│         FINDING NEMO (G)                 │
│       (11:40  3:25  5:20) 7:45           │
│           MATILDA (PG)                   │
│       (12:45  3:50) 6:55  10:00          │
└─────────────────────────────────────────┘
```

1. Which movie starts the earliest? _____

2. How many times is each movie shown? ____

3. Which movies are rated G? _____

4. What time is the last showing of *Matilda*?

   _____

5. When does the last bargain show play?

   _____

Study Hall

1. Number these movies in alphabetical order.

   _____ *Matilda*   _____ *Titanic*

   _____ *Shrek*   _____ *Big*

   _____ *Mulan*   _____ *Superman*

   _____ *Goonies*   _____ *Babe*

   _____ *Tarzan*   _____ *Antz*

The Great *Titanic*

Do you believe a boat can be unsinkable?

Traveling by sea was popular one hundred years ago. Many people crossed the ocean to come to America. Others sailed on vacations. Some ships were like hotels. They had dining rooms, game rooms, and swimming pools. The most famous ship was the *Titanic*.

The *Titanic* was almost 900 yards long. That is as long as three football fields. It had several floors called <u>decks</u>. On the lowest floor, men shoveled coal into furnaces. The fires helped power the ship. On the top floor was a lounge. Passengers could relax there. The ship even had elevators. People said nothing could sink the *Titanic*.

The *Titanic* sailed from England in 1912. About 2,000 people were on the ship. Many rich people were onboard. Some of them brought their pets. But some people used most of their money just to buy a ticket. These people wanted to live in America. They stayed in the section called Third Class. Third Class was in the lower part of the ship. The bedrooms were nice but not luxurious.

The *Titanic* sailed on the Atlantic through blocks of ice. Ice broken off a glacier is an <u>iceberg</u>. Icebergs are as hard as rocks. One Sunday night, a boatman saw something in the darkness. "Iceberg right ahead!" he called out. But it was too late. The ship struck the iceberg. Ice fell on the deck. Young boys even played with it.

The iceberg ripped a hole in the ship. Water began pouring in. The captain told his men to get the lifeboats ready. These small boats held about 50 people. More and more water rushed in. Workers ran from the water. Other passengers did not know the ship was sinking. Most lifeboats left only partly full. One girl was even able to save her dog.

The great *Titanic* sank. It went under the water two and a half hours after hitting the iceberg. Seven hundred people were saved, but 1,500 people died. Many brave people died after saving their friends or family. The tragedy of the *Titanic* will never be forgotten.

©RBP Books　　　www.summerbridgeactivities.com　　　Reading Connection—Grade 3—RBP3829

Read and Think

Circle the correct answer.

1. What is the main idea of this passage?
   A. Traveling by sea was popular a hundred years ago.
   B. Traveling by ship is dangerous.
   C. The sinking of the *Titanic* was a tragedy.

2. Mark an **X** in the blank if it is a detail about the *Titanic*.

   _____ nothing could sink it

   _____ it had a lounge

   _____ the lifeboats held 50 people

   _____ it was 900 feet long

   _____ the ship sailed in 1915

   _____ people brought pets on board

   _____ it was like a hotel

   _____ it took two and a half hours to sink

Circle the correct answer.

3. The *Titanic* sank because
   A. it was too heavy.
   B. of the cold weather.
   C. it hit an iceberg.

Word Attack

Write the number of the synonym in the blank.

1. boat   _____ struck

2. delay   _____ deck

3. floor   _____ late

4. sink   _____ fall

5. hit   _____ ship

Underline the three words that belong.

6. pool   lounge   elevator   fountain

7. workers   pets   passengers   people

8. ocean   water   sea   ice

9. football   coal   swimming   sailing

Study Hall

Put an **X** by the word that would be on the same page as the guidewords.

1. effective/elevate

   ___ elevators   ___ elegant   ___ eliminate

2. tiger/tractor

   ___ *Titanic*   ___ tragedy   ___ travel

3. amaze/athlete

   ___ Atlantic   ___ ahead   ___ America

4. faint/famine

   ___ football   ___ family   ___ famous

5. simple/sudden

   ___ swimming   ___ sea   ___ sink

Reading Connection—Grade 3—RBP3829   www.summerbridgeactivities.com   ©RBP Books

Answer Pages

Page 8

Read and Think
1. A
2. B
3. C

Try to Apply
1. talk about your feelings
   take some time to calm down
   take a deep breath

Word Attack
1. laugh   cry
   love   hate
   work   rest
   give   get
   sad   happy
2. Answers will vary.
3. command

Page 10

Read and Think
1. C
2. A
3. (!), (.);   (.), (!);   (!), (.)
   Sentences will vary.

Try to Apply
1. Answers will vary.

Word Attack
1. ordinary
2. A

Study Hall
1. encyclopedia
   a children's book about outside activities

Page 12

Read and Think
1. A
2. 5, 1, 2, 4, 3
3. A
4. pulling my leg   teasing me
   hit the road   get going
   talked my ear off   talked too much
   shoot the breeze   talk about nothing
                         in particular
   time flies   time passes quickly

Try to Apply
1. Answers will vary.

Word Attack
1. begged
2. logging
3. cutting
4. walks
5. times
6. day

Page 14

Read and Think
1. B
2. 3, 5, 1, 4, 2
3. C
4. B
5. C

Language Skills
1. Kate and Nicole
2. bubbles
3. Nicole
4. bubble
5. Dad

Word Attack
1. large
2. girls
3. inside
4. back
5. stronger

www.summerbridgeactivities.com
Reading Connection—Grade 3—RBP3829

Answer Pages

Page 16

Read and Think
1. B
2. C
3. A
4. C
5. Answers will vary.

Study Hall
1. 4
2. 2
3. 1
4. 11

Language Skills
1. Jen
2. Marie
3. Jen

Page 18

Read and Think
1. C
2. B
3. A. He is too young.
   B. He can't drive.
   C. He has no money.
4. He has wandered or run away from home.
   (Answers may vary.)

Word Attack
1. C, B
2. B, C
3. B, C
4. B, C

Study Hall
1. 4 8
   7 5
   2 1
   3 6
2. 2 2
   5 3
   4 4
   4 3

Page 20

Read and Think
1. B
2. F, T, F, F, T, T
3. A
4. A. milk
   B. candy bar
   C. cheese

Try to Apply
1. Answers will vary.

Language Skills
1. are, <u>needed</u>
2. be, <u>eaten</u>
3. can, <u>make</u>
4. You need all kinds of food to be healthy.
5. These provide protein to make the body strong.

Page 22

Read and Think
1. C
2. B
3. B

Word Attack
1. hobbyhorse
2. blacksmith
3. nickname
4. boneshakers
5. someone
6. rearview

7. end
8. best
9. funny
10. stop
11. filled
12. many
13. cheap
14. someone

Language Skills
1-2. Answers will vary.

144

Answer Pages

Page 24

Read and Think
1. C
2. F, F, T, T, T
3. The rules help keep you safe.

Word Attack
1. A. brakes, B. sense, C. pedals

Language Skills
1. properly
2. easily
3. closely

Word Attack
1. motorcycle
2. shoelaces
3. handlebars
4. racetrack

Try to Apply
1. Answers will vary.

Page 26

Read and Think

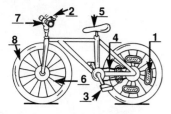

Answers will vary, but should include:
9. If you don't know how to stop, you might crash.
10. You might be hit by a car if you don't signal to let others know where you are going.
11. You might lose control of your bike and fall or crash.

Word Attack
1. b
2. b
3. a
4. b
5. b

Try to Apply
1. Answers will vary.

Page 28

Read and Think
1. Heroes choose to act selflessly.
   Heroes give it their all.
   Heroes keep trying.
   Heroes go the extra mile.
2. A
3. Answers will vary.
4. B
5. B

Word Attack
1. give
2. stop
3. day
4. all
5. answer
6. go
7. more

Language Skills
1. Heroes (circle) make (X) <u>mistakes</u>.
2. They (circle) answer (X) <u>the call</u>.
3. Heroes (circle) seize (X) <u>the day</u>.
4. We (circle) go (X) <u>the extra mile</u>.
5. Heroes (circle) treat (X) <u>others kindly</u>.

Page 30

Read and Think
1. B
2. F, T, T, T
3. B
4. C

Word Attack
1. A. k, gh B. k, w C. k
   D. e E. e F. e
2. combat
3. served
4. symbol
5. worn
6. knock

Language Skills
1. their
2. His
3. his
4. her
5. our
6. my/your

Answer Pages

Page 32

Read and Think
1. C
2. C
3. A

Word Attack
1. A. join as one
   B. Answers will vary.
      Examples: unicorn, unify, universe, unicycle, uniform
2. A mer i can
3. con tri bu tion
4. at tend ed
5. in de pen dence
6. rep re sent ing
7. al le giance

Study Hall
1. 5, 7-9, 22
2. 6, 28-30
3. 19, 25

Try to Apply
1. Answers will vary.

Page 34

Read and Think
1. A
2. He wrote books and newspaper articles.
   He helped to write the Declaration of Independence.
   He discovered facts about electricity.
3. 5, 4, 2, 1, 3

Try to Apply
1. Answer will vary.

Word Attack
1. inventor
2. printer
3. writer
4. helper

Language Skills
1. He invented a type of glasses because he wanted to be able to read in his old age.
2. He helped start the first fire station after a fire destroyed much of Philadelphia.
3. He is still an American hero today, although he died on April 17, 1790.

Page 36

Read and Think
1. B
2. A
3. A
4.
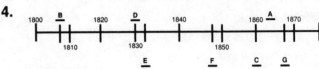

Word Attack
1. pres i dent
2. leg is la ture
3. rep re sen ta tive
4. E man ci pa tion Proc la ma tion
5. Get tys burg Ad dress

Language Skills
1. Slavery was a major problem in the Civil War.
2. The Gettysburg Address was a famous speech given by President Lincoln.
3. Honest Abe Lincoln united the divided country.

Page 38

Read and Think
1. B
2. 3, 5, 1, 4, 2

Word Attack
1. graduate
   celebrate
   demonstrate
   segregate
2. graduate   to complete learning requirements
   celebrate   to praise
   demonstrate   to protest against
   segregate   to separate
3. A
4. C

Try to Apply
1. Answers will vary.

Language Skills
1. taught
2. gave
3. shot
4. spoke

Answer Pages

Page 40

Read and Think

3	1	5	4	6	2
1903	1971	1984	1996	1998	1999

Word Attack
1. win
2. swim
3. athlete
4. expect
5. survive
6. ride

Language Skills
1. yellow
2. steep or great
3. broken
4. top

Try to Apply
1–3. Answers will vary.

Page 42

Read and Think
1. They helped Georgie and called 911 for Mrs. Stevens.
2. A
3. You only call 911 in an emergency.

Word Attack
1. synonym
2. antonym
3. synonym
4. antonym
5. antonym
6. synonym

Try to Apply
1. Answers will vary.

Language Skills
1. was
2. is
3. are
4. were
5. am

Page 44

Read and Think
1. Answers will vary.
2. 1, 6, 2, 3, 4, 5
3. B
4. C
5. C

Word Attack
1. take — took
2. become — became
3. bring — brought
4. begin — began
5. go — went
6. C
7. A

Language Skills (Answers may vary.)
1. Our cat smelled smoke, and he tried to wake us.
2. Mom takes in stray animals and gives them a bath.
3. The cat tried to wake up mom, dad, and me.

Page 46

Read and Think
1. A
2. A

Word Attack
1. land — sea
   ground — sky
   wild — tame
   few — many
   small — tall
2. animals, ants, giraffes, mammals, insects, reptiles, amphibians, cows, birds, trees

Try to Apply
1. whale
2. giraffe
3. dog
4. snake
5. rabbit
6. Answers will vary.

Language Skills (Answers may vary.)
1. Is this a never-ending game?
2. Do some animals fly and some walk?
3. You can name many animals.

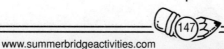

www.summerbridgeactivities.com   Reading Connection—Grade 3—RBP3829

Answer Pages

Page 48

Read and Think
1. B
2. F, T, F, T
3. elephant   in groups
   otter   floating on its back
   bat   upside down
   flamingo   standing on one foot
   squirrel   in nests in trees

Word Attack
1. C

Language Skills
1. s'   3. 's
2. s'   4. 's

Study Hall
1. 20   3. 11
2. 10   4. 26

Try to Apply
1. Answers will vary.

Page 50

Read and Think
1. A
2. feathers
3. teeth
4. eggs
5. nests
6. 3, 2, 1, 4
7. F, T, T, F, F

Word Attack
1. B
2. fly
3. watch
4. own

Language Skills
1. fly
2. eat
3. build
4. hatch
5. teach

Page 52

Read and Think
1. B
2. F, T, T, F, F
3.

	ostrich	other birds
cannot fly	X	
has feathers	X	X
lays eggs	X	X
grows to be eight feet tall	X	
protective of its young	X	X

Word Attack
1. eight
2. two
3. weigh
4. male
5. C
6. –er
7. –est
8. –est
9. –est

Page 54

Read and Think
1. Seahorses are interesting sea animals.
2. egg
3. mouth
4. male
5. female   pouch
6. A is not true.

Word Attack
1. A. seahorses
   B. fins
   C. babies
   D. pouches
   E. bodies
2. A. sea   horse
   B. up   right
   C. sea   weed
   D. new   born
   E. with   in

Study Hall
1. snout, seaweed
2. egg

Answer Pages

Page 56

Read and Think
1. C
2. M: cat, tiger, giraffe, leopard
   N: octopus, fish, owl, robin, alligator

Mind Buster
Answers will vary.

Word Attack
1. The body temperature remains the same regardless of the outside temperature.
2. omnivores
3. carnivores
4. insectivores
5. herbivores
6. long a spelled a consonant e: shapes, whale, same
7. long a spelled ay: ways, stays
8. long i spelled i consonant e: sizes, time, live, like, outside
9. long i spelled y: fly, sky

Page 58

Read and Think
1. C
2. driver ant
3. spiders, frogs, insects
4. queen, worker, soldier
5. 3, 1, 2, 4
6. B

Language Skills
1. I   2. C   3. I
4. I   5. C   6. C

Study Hall
1. 8   2. 1   3. 15
4. 15   5. 1

Page 60

Read and Think
1. A
2. B
3. B
4. 2, 1, 3

Word Attack
1. high
2. made
3. No
4. scene

Language Skills
1. head driver ant
2. surviving worms
3. High and Mighty: first, deserving, prideful
   Worm: lowly, poor, wriggly

Page 62

Read and Think
1. C
2. B

Word Attack
1. B

Try to Apply
1. Because he went to Hollywood
2. Answers will vary.

Language Skills
1. Some
2. strange
3. first
4. animal
5. second
6. Hollywood's peculiar habit
7. reporter's article
8. animals' tricks
9. Hollywood's movie

© RBP Books   www.summerbridgeactivities.com   Reading Connection—Grade 3—RBP3829

Answer Pages

Page 64

Read and Think
1. Answers will vary.
2. C
3. Answers will vary.

Word Attack
1. B
2. dry, fly, sky
3. white
4. high, sight

Language Skills
1. N
2. Y
3. N
4. N
5. N
6. tall
7. bright, arid

Page 66

Read and Think
1. B
2. Answers will vary.
3. F, T, T, F, F
4. B
5. B

Try to Apply
1. Answers will vary.

Word Attack
1. pros/per/ous
2. coun/tries
3. im/mi/gra/tion
4. in/spec/tion
5. dis/ap/point/ed
6. A/mer/i/cans
7. en/trance
8. of/fi/cers

9. find
10. passed
11. giving
12. entered

Page 68

Read and Think
1. B
2. T, F, T, T, F
3. A
4. B
5. C

Word Attack
1. enormous, huge, gigantic, large, colossal, immense
2. A, B

Language Skills
1. I can't believe the statue weighed 225 tons!
2. The Statue of Liberty stands for freedom for all.

Page 70

Read and Think
1. C
2. to find wealth and prosperity
3. They stayed in China to care for the children and take care of the farms.
4. A

Word Attack
1. did   not
2. was   not
3. were   not
4. could   not
5. living
6. digging
7. striking
8. paying
9. earning

Language Skills
1. are, P
2. was, S
3. were, P
4. was, S
5. is, S

Answer Pages

Page 72

Read and Think
1. A
2. B
3. A. China
   B. laundry service
   C. ship
   D. grandfather
4. A

Word Attack
1. grand   father
2. paper   work
3. bed   room
4. grand   mother

Language Skills
1. because
2. while
3. although
4. until
5. after

Try to Apply
Answers will vary.

Page 74

Read and Think
1. F
2. T
3. F
4. T
5. T

Word Attack
1. favorite
2. whole
3. stand
4. orbit
5. va/ca/tion
6. grand/moth/er
7. emp/er/or
8. con/nect/ed
9. as/tro/nauts

Language Skills
1. my family
2. the emperor
3. the wall
4. the watchtowers

Page 76

Read and Think
1. 4, 1, 2, 3
2. C
3. T
4. T
5. F
6. T
7. F

Word Attack
1. 1, 4, 5, 2, 3, 6

Language Skills
1. V   5. V
2. V   6. N
3. N   7. N
4. N   8. V

Page 78

Read and Think
1. A. partnering
   B. swimming in schools
   C. camouflage
2. C
3. C

Word Attack
1. er   2. est
3. clam, marlin, anemone
4. swim, walk, ride
5. live   9. clean
6. laugh   10. swim
7. strike   11. amaze
8. sting   12. kid

Study Hall
1. p. 42
2. p. 37–38
3. coral

www.summerbridgeactivities.com   Reading Connection—Grade 3—RBP3829

Answer Pages

Page 80

Read and Think
1. Great Wall
2. Great Wall
3. Barrier Reef
4. Barrier Reef
5. Great Wall
6. Both
7. Barrier Reef
8. Both
9. Barrier Reef
10. Great Wall
11. Both
12. Barrier Reef
13. Great Wall
14. Barrier Reef
15. Great Wall
16. Both

Venn Diagram
Great Wall—man-made wonder, 4,500 miles long, found on land, many men died building this, 1,000 years to build, ten-men wide

Great Barrier Reef—45 miles wide, billions of polyps died to make this, natural wonder, 1,200 miles long, 1,000,000 years old, found in the ocean

Same—built in sections, seen from space, visited by tourists, endangered

Page 82

Read and Think
1. C
2. Georgia and Alabama
3. A. flowers
   B. southeastern
   C. Spanish
   D. fruit and fruit juices
4. B

Word Attack
1. southeast
   grapefruit
   sunshine

Language Skills
1. N, V
2. V, N
3. V, N
4. V, N
5. N, V

Page 84

Read and Think
1. A
2. Answers will vary.
3. Answers may vary.
   A. people, animals, food, rides
   B. animals, barkers
   C. animals, hot dogs, cotton candy
   D. animals, food
   E. hot dogs, cotton candy, drinks
4. A

Word Attack
1. air; there, answers will vary
2. fed; answers will vary
3. fly; answers will vary
4. today; answers will vary
5. noise(s)
6. lucky
7. fast
8. love

Language Skills
1. heard
2. felt
3. spun
4. sold
5. went

Page 86

Read and Think
1. B
2. C
3. one month
4. A
5. F
6. F
7. O

Language Skills
1. cherries—fresh, canned, frozen
2. pie crust—thick, dough, puffy, flakier, big
3. pie—cherry, sweet, tart, first place, best, prize

Word Attack
1. cherries
2. pies
3. crusts
4. flakier
5. doughier
6. decided
7. better, best
8. flakier, flakiest
9. sweeter, sweetest
10. thicker, thickest
11. puffier, puffiest

Answer Pages

Page 88

Read and Think
1. A
2. F, T, T, T
3. piglet   baby pig
   sow   mother pig
   litter   a group of baby pigs from one mother
   nuzzled   cuddled
   raised   to help grow up
4. B
5. C

Study Hall
1. 2
2. 1
3. 1
4. 2
5. 2
6. 1

Try to Apply
Answers will vary.

Page 90

Read and Think
1. a roller coaster
2. a snake
3. C

Word Attack
1. i
2. a
3. n o
4. u
5. S
6. A
7. S
8. A
9. S
10. S
11. wh
12. gh
13. th
14. sh

Try to Apply
1. Answers will vary.

Page 92

Read and Think
1. B
2. C

Try to Apply
1. make-believe

Word Attack
1. B, A, C, D, F, E
2. read, sea, dream
3. me, be, we
4. free, seeking, seem
5. away, play
6. sail
7. tale, places
8. time, hide

Page 94

Read and Think
1. B
2. C

Word Attack
1. warmer
2. happier
3. shorter or longer
4. older
5. higher
6. warmest
7. happiest
8. shortest
9. oldest
10. highest

Try to Apply
1. She would melt.
2. Sentences will vary.
3. Sentences will vary.

Answer Pages

Page 96

Read and Think
1. B
2. 2, 5, 1, 4, 3
3. A

Try to Apply
1. make-believe
2. Answers will vary.

Word Attack
1. whenever
2. something
3. cupboard
4. blueberry
5. into
6. pour
7. bare
8. daze
9. grate
10. ate

Page 98

Read and Think
1. If fairy tales were real, life would be strange.

Try to Apply
1. Answers will vary.
2. glass slipper
3. magic mirror
4. poison apple
5. talking fish
6. wicked stepsister
7. Answers will vary.

Word Attack
1. slay, play
2. whale, tale
3. strange
4. twice
5. pebbles
6. frogs
7. porridge
8. meal
9. bind
10. talk
11. nice

Page 100

Read and Think
1. At the pet shop.
2. Grandma hasn't seen Poochy since she stopped at that shop.
3. B
4. 4, 2, 1, 3, 5

Try to Apply
1. the ice cream store

Word Attack
1. forget   remember
   east   west
   north   south
   left   right
   lost   found
   large   small

Language Skills (Answers may vary.)
1. She, find, glasses
2. Grandmother, lost, dog
3. girl, tie, outside
4. I, sat, bench

Page 102

Read and Think
1. Italy
2. Canada
3. France
4. Africa

Try to Apply
1. Answers will vary.

Language Skills
1. ?
2. (.)
3. !
4. (.)
5. !
6. sends
7. flew
8. tells
9. Give
10. saw

Answer Pages

Page 104

Read and Think
1. The correct counselor is the fourth from the left.
2. F, F, T, F, T
3. B

Try to Apply
1–3. Answers will vary.
4. The counselors all looked similar.

Word Attack
1. who   is
2. was   not
3. you   will
4. I   will
5. I   am

Language Skills
1. left
2. find
3. wrote
4. thought
5. got

Page 106

Read and Think
1. The correct prince is the first on the left.
2. He has eight buttons instead of seven.
3. T, T, F, F, T

Word Attack
1. gentle   men
2. up   set
3. hand   book
4. god   mother
5. wrist   watch

Try to Apply
1. Answers will vary.

Language Skills
1. gentlemen (circle), greet, Cinderella (X over)
2. prince (circle), wearing, crown (X over)
3. She (circle), read, book (X over)
4. shirt (circle), had, buttons (X over)

Word Attack
1. ugly
2. last
3. lose
4. forget

Page 108

Read and Think
1. A. taco
   B. chicken
   C. pizza (or hamburger)
   D. hamburger (or pizza)
2. C
3. Brad. He would only eat chicken.
4. 5, 4, 2, 1, 3

Try to Apply
1-2. Answers will vary.

Word Attack
1. B
2. stro ga noff
3. la sa gna
4. cas se role
5. zuc chi ni
6. bur ri tos
7. ham bur ger
8. gua ca mo le
9. ome e let

Language Skills
Answers will vary.

Page 110

Read and Think
1. B
2. F, T, F, F, T
3. Martin left the doors open.
4. Cage 1: dog, Cage 2: cat
   Cage 3: hamster, Cage 4: rabbit
5. goldfish, turtle, crab
6. gerbil, hamster, mouse
7. cricket, tarantula, ant
8. kitten, puppy, duckling

Word Attack
1. A. help B. take C. do D. clean E. care
2. mice
3. deer
4. cattle/cows
5. moose
6. oxen
7. geese
8. wolves

www.summerbridgeactivities.com   Reading Connection—Grade 3—RBP3829

Answer Pages

Page 112

Language Skills
1. My
2. her
3. his
4. their
5. your

Word Attack
1. We look a lot alike.
2. Would you please listen to me?
3. It was really raining hard.
4. autumn
5. to agree
6. to join two ends of ribbon
7. a journey
8. a piece of metal used to open a lock

Page 114

Read and Think
1. put a sock in it
   lollygag all night
   dead to the world
   kept their eyes peeled
   jumped out of their skin

Word Attack
1. little
2. skin
3. antsy
4. lollygag

Try to Apply
1–2. Answers will vary.

Page 116

Read and Think
1. 3, 2, 1
2. 2, 1, 3
3. B

Word Attack
1. rubbing
2. experiment
3. point
4. create, build
5. correct, right
6. bar, rod
7. small, thin

Try to Apply
1–11. Answers will vary.

Page 118

Read and Think
1. F
2. O
3. F
4. O
5. F
6. A
7. C

Word Attack
1. C
2. B

Language Skills
1. exciting trip
2. muddy pools
3. black beaches
4. kiwi house
5. bossy personalities

Answer Pages

Page 120

Read and Think
1. F
2. T
3. F
4. T
5. F
6. 3, 2, 1, 4

Language Skills
1. humpback whales
2. whales
3. album

Try to Apply
1–5. Answers will vary.

Page 122

Read and Think
1. C
2. B
3. A

Study Hall
1. no
2. no
3. yes
4. preheat
5. peak
6. cream of tartar
7. 1, 5, 4, 3, 6, 2

Page 124

Read and Think
1. C
2. 4, 1, 2, 3
3. F, F, F, T

Study Hall
1. Famous Fliers
2. Aviation Today
3. 56
4. 6 or 22
5. How Do Planes Fly?

Mind Buster
Answers will vary.

Page 126

Read and Think
1. B
2. C
3. C
4. B

Word Attack
1. all
2. inn
3. for
4. no
5. one
6. wrapped
7. side
8. be
9. would

Study Hall
1. devoted, door
2. misfortune, mats, mirror
3. scattered, sleep, station
4. rabbi

Language Skills
1. was <u>traveling</u>
2. had <u>scattered</u>
3. was <u>hurrying</u>
4. have <u>slept</u>

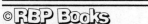

Answer Pages

Page 128

Read and Think
1. B
2. B
3. B
4. B
5. A
6. C

Language Skills
1. turtle, elephant, kangaroo
2. hopping, running, traveling
3. seat, trunk, tires
4. sleep
5. trip
6. big
7. mind

Try to Apply
Answers will vary.

Page 130

Read and Think
1. F
2. O
3. F
4. O
5. O
6. A
7. B

Language Skills
1. The king of France and two brothers
2. A major in the army and a physics professor
3. Ed Yost and Raven Industries
4. Ed Yost and the Navy
5. think
6. do
7. begin
8. lose
9. sell

Mind Buster
Answers will vary.

Page 132

Read and Think
1. C
2. A
3. F
4. F
5. O
6. O

Language Skills
1. their, animals
2. her, Sassy
3. his, Luath
4. my, Peter

Word Attack
1. pet's
2. friend's
3. lab's
4. book's

Page 134

Read and Think
1. B
2. C
3. C

Word Attack
incorrect, unlucky, unbelief, disbelief, discontent, unhappy, unsafe, unbelievable

Language Skills
1. were
2. was/had
3. had
4. has
5. is/was
6. cat
7. paws
8. home
9. miles
10. pet
11. shelter

Mind Buster
Answers will vary.

Answer Pages

Page 136

Read and Think
1. B
2. B
3. A
4. 7, 4, 5, 3, 1, 6, 2

Mind Buster (Answers will vary.)
Soyuz 1, April 23, 1967
Apollo 1, January 27, 1967
Soyuz 11, June 6, 1971
Challenger, January 28, 1986
Columbia, February 1, 2003

Study Hall
1. C
2. A
3. A
4. C

Page 138

Read and Think
1. C
2. B
3. 5, 1, 2, 3, 4

Word Attack
1. flew
2. all
3. weak

Study Hall
1. It was a tragedy that so many people died on September 11, 2001.
2. B
3. A

Language Skills
1. Our class had a visitor.
2. Why is the passenger pigeon extinct?
3. There was no place left to build a nest.

Page 140

Read and Think
1. F
2. O
3. O
4. F
5. F
6. Suddenly, a phone booth appears.
7. The boys will be in different places.
8. It will be really funny.

Try to Apply
1. *Finding Nemo*
2. 4
3. *The Rookie; Finding Nemo*
4. 10:00
5. 5:20

Study Hall
1. 5, 7, 6, 4, 9
   10, 3, 8, 2, 1

Page 142

Read and Think
1. C
2. it had a lounge; the lifeboats held 50 people; people brought pets on board; it was like a hotel; it took two and a half hours to sink
3. C

Word Attack
1. 5 struck
2. 3 deck
3. 2 late
4. 4 fall
5. 1 ship

6. pool, lounge, elevator
7. workers, passengers, people
8. ocean, water, sea
9. football, swimming, sailing

Study Hall
1. elegant
2. Titanic
3. America
4. family
5. sink

Notes

Five things I'm thankful for:

1. _____
2. _____
3. _____
4. _____
5. _____